Behavior Modification

A Practical Guide for Teachers

by James A. Poteet

HODDER AND STOUGHTON
LONDON SYDNEY AUCKLAND TORONTO

ISBN 0 340 18499 X

Printed and bound in Great Britain for
Hodder and Stoughton Educational,
a division of Hodder and Stoughton Ltd.,
Mill Road, Dunton Green, Sevenoaks, Kent,
by Unwin Brothers Limited,
The Gresham Press, Old Woking,
Surrey, England.

Foreword

This is a book for teachers and intending teachers. It appears at a time when its theme, behaviour modification, is one of the growth points in educational psychology.

Many observers have commented on the undue emphasis which is often placed on the study of intellectual behaviour. One of the reasons for the growth of interest in behaviour modification is its relevance to all kinds of behaviour— social and emotional behaviour, for example, as well as intellectual behaviour. Indeed most of the studies mentioned in this book are concerned with non-intellectual behaviour of the kind that all teachers meet.

The established teacher may feel that he has developed his own skills of class control and behaviour modification. But to the student teacher and to the concerned and enquiring practitioner, the management of classroom behaviour, and not merely its study, is an area of major interest. This is another reason why behaviour modification is a growth point in educational psychology. Not only do behaviour modification studies relate to this area of teaching skill, but they also offer to teachers techniques which can be of direct use in the classroom.

But practical suggestions are often seductive. What works for one teacher may not work for another: each situation is unique. One of the merits of this text is

① Related to psychology

that its proposals can be worked through and tried out in the classroom. Its content lends itself to evaluation. Although the book is written in an easy—even colloquial—style, it is American and the British reader occasionally has to translate the American terminology into its British equivalent. This, however, is not a major problem. And if some of the illustrations of the management of classroom behaviour seem alien in the British educational context, they will also provoke discussion—which is all to the good. More discussion is sure to be stimulated by the range of studies that the author has quoted. Dr Poteet has been careful to include studies which cover a variety of age-ranges, for example, and the variations of behaviour and reinforcement illustrated by them will be useful starting-points for debate.

Although the book is based on research material it does not pretend to deal thoroughly with the underlying theory: other texts must be consulted for this. As the sub-title suggests, it is a book which emphasizes the practical. For this reason alone it will go a long way to meet a criticism which is sometimes levelled at courses of initial training, namely that they over-emphasize the theoretical and that they are more concerned with managing the academic material than the human material of the teaching situation.

The student needs to be alerted to the warning expressed in the book itself, that the learning theory which underlies behaviour modification cannot be expected to be the sole answer to all behaviour problems. Given this, the content will provide useful and interesting material for any introductory course seeking to teach the ideas of behaviour modification in an educational context.

Phillip Williams
The Open University, 1973

Contents

CHAPTER I

Describing Behavior

THIS BOOK WAS NOT written to be quickly skimmed in a few hours. It was written for the purpose of guiding you, a teacher, through a process of changing the behavior of one or more of your students in your classroom. To achieve this purpose, chances are that you, too, will have to modify your own behavior so that it will "fit in" to the approach you will use.

This book WAS written for you to read, reread, and at appropriate times in the future, to read again. As your behavior gradually accommodates to the ground rules expressed in this book, you will find that you are more positive in your outlook on teaching, you seem more patient, and you experience fewer problems in individual and classroom management.

Sounds good, doesn't it?

Let's begin this adventure. The first thing to do is to give a few minutes of thought to your classroom and to the behavior of the students in it. Try to picture the situation as though you were a visitor to your room who does not know you or the students. Pause after each of the following questions in order to mentally see your classroom, and then answer the question to yourself:

– Is the room attractive?
– How are the desks arranged?

1

  — Are materials easily accessible?
  — What is the noise level?
  — Do students seem free to come and go as they please?
  — Is there too much movement around the room?
  — Do the students seem to watch the teacher?
  — Does the teacher move around while talking?
  — Do only a few students answer questions?
  — What are the noninvolved students doing?

Spend a few more minutes watching your classroom in your mind's eye.

I hope you were pleased with what you saw. There were probably some things that you would like to see changed. Jot them down below:

_____

_____

_____

_____

_____

_____

You probably saw a few individual students whose behavior was not what you would like. In your mind's eye look at them again in the classroom. Look carefully — look at each student, one at a time. Does he (or she):

  — speak out of turn?
  — interrupt?
  — not raise his hand?
  — come to your desk too frequently?
  — seem too quiet and withdrawn?
  — not turn in his assignments?
  — seem incapable of working independently?
  — fight too often?
  — make trouble on the playground?
  — mark any answer just to finish the worksheet?

Jot down the names of those students who are of most concern to you:

_____

_____

_____

_____

In order to get a better picture of the total environment in which you work, pause after each of these questions and answer them to yourself:

- Who is your best teacher friend?
- What subject or grade level does your friend teach?
- Do you ever share your good days with your teacher friend?
- Do you ever plan in a cooperative manner with other teachers to give assistance to a certain student?
- What happens when you and your teacher friend disagree?
- Do you get any compliments?
- How do you get along with the principal?
- Does he listen to your suggestions?
- Are the rules of your school strict or lenient?
- Do they make any sense?
- Do you know how far you can go in doing something different?
- Will the principal let you be creative in and out of the classroom?
- What topics are discussed in the teacher's lounge?
- Is the general feeling of the school free and relaxed or is it uptight?

The purpose of the preceding was to give you the opportunity to see your own teaching style and instructional environment.

Your task now is to give serious consideration to one student whose behavior, in some way, you would like to see changed. Give a few moments to select THE student of most concern. Write a complete description of the problem situation below.

Name of Student _____ Age _____

Problem:

State what you think are the causes of the problem:

State what you are doing to try to solve the problem:

For those of you who are having a difficult time finding a "problem" to describe, a few comments might be in order.

While you are concerned with academic achievement, you are probably also concerned about other behavior students exhibit in the classroom. Do you know a student who can't seem to get down to work, who doesn't finish his work on time, who stares out of the window, who asks you for help too often, etc.? It is this type of behavior that you probably want to modify because it is not productive behavior.

But there is also the more obvious behavior that appears to express hostility and aggression. You are concerned about this behavior probably to a greater degree than the quieter type of behavior because not only is it nonproductive for the student, but it keeps you from doing your best job in the classroom. It disrupts the class.

When given the opportunity to choose any type of behavior to modify, most teachers choose to work first on behavior that disrupts the class. This is understandable since the teacher is responsible for the education of about thirty students all in the same room at the same time.

Just what does *disruptive* behavior mean? Some teachers have defined *disruptive* behavior to mean talking out, being loud or making unnecessary noise, being out of seat without permission, etc. If such behavior occurs frequently, it certainly is easy to understand why most teachers would want to modify it in order to get down to the business of teaching instead of spending so much time disciplining disruptive students.

The more openly hostile behavior is termed *aggressive* behavior. It has been defined as physically attacking another person such as is seen in fighting, biting, shoving, hitting, etc. (Poteet, 1971). While this aggressive behavior might be considered quite serious, it is usually the disruptive type of behavior that is of concern to most teachers probably because it occurs more frequently and is sustained by more students than that of open hostility. Interestingly enough, most disruptive behavior is displayed by boys rather than by girls.

Since you have written what you think are the causes of your student's behavior, you might be interested in what other teachers have stated as causes of the problems they expressed. By far, the most prevalent cause was attributed to the home environment. Some of the specific causes listed were: broken home, no home supervision, working parents, insufficient parent attention, extreme methods of punishment by parents, very strict parents, being an only child, death of a parent, etc. Other reasons given were: low IQ, a need for attention, not enough challenge, hyperactivity, emotional problems, etc. − a variety of reasons, to say the least.

What were other teachers doing about the problems? No single approach was favored over any other. They changed the seating arrangement, were tolerant and gave out love and understanding, threatened, yelled and lectured, had parent conferences, used special materials, individualized instruction, talked to the problem student, referred him to psychological services, etc. If you are teaching, you probably have done most, if not all of these things to attempt to solve a problem you have had. If you have, you are a lot like other teachers. The problem, however, is that often we still have the problem after we have taken the above actions.

SPECIFY THE BEHAVIOR

Getting back to the task of describing the problem, consider this description given by a teacher:

This year's class is one of the worst I have ever had. There are two boys who really bother me, and I simply don't know what to do about them. One of them, Eddie, is really something! He is so noisy. Not a minute goes by without that boy making some kind of noise. Not just noise, but *loud* noise. He's extremely disrespectful, not only to me but to everybody in the room. On top of that, he is constantly on-the-go. I've never seen a kid that was so active.

Sound familiar?

Sure it does. You probably have had an Eddie in your classroom before or have one now.

Let's look at some of the key words the teacher used to describe Eddie: NOISY, LOUD, DISRESPECTFUL, ON-THE-GO. Jot down what these words meant to you as you read the teacher's description of Eddie:

NOISY: _____

_____

LOUD: _____

_____

DISRESPECTFUL: _____

_____

ON-THE-GO: _____

_____

A group of teachers were asked to do this same task. Here are a few of their meanings:

NOISY	LOUD	DISRESPECTFUL	ON-THE-GO
— rattles papers	— speaks out	— sasses	— very active
— not sure of self	— boyish	— mouthy	— can't sit still
— bored	— drops things	— doesn't listen	— discontented
— wants attention	— wants attention	— attention seeking	— work is too hard
— lacks self-respect	— hostile	— resentment	— feels inadequate
— thumps desk	— spoiled	— hyperactive	— hyperactive

Now compare what you wrote with what other teachers wrote. You probably were like some of the other teachers and not like others. Many different meanings to the same word (i.e., NOISY) were expressed. Yet, you, as well as the other teachers, all agreed that the description of Eddie sounded very familiar.

Isn't it now obvious that a behavior description given by one person does not necessarily mean the same thing to someone else?

Wouldn't it be a good idea to decide more accurately what it is we are talking about when we describe a student's behavior?

Good description of behavior requires objectivity on the part of the observer, the person doing the describing. Being objective takes practice to develop. Watch a student (or any other person) for two or three minutes. Tell yourself *exactly* what he does. You might be amazed at how many different things he actually does in such a short amount of time.

After you think you are fairly objective in your observation skills, watch someone and write down what he does. Did you note what hand the person used? Which foot did he use on the first step? Did he make any pauses in movement? Did he glance up or down? It would be interesting to give your description to someone else and ask him to act out what he reads. You may then find that your description was not as complete or objective as you thought.

There are probably many different definitions of behavior. For our purposes, *behavior* is what someone does that we can see. It must be defined or described in such a way that you, as well as others, know precisely what you are talking about. It must be defined *specifically* in such a way that if another teacher would observe the same behavior, she would be able to tell you when it occurred and be in *complete* agreement with you.

LABEL THE BEHAVIOR

The behavior should first be labeled. Take the student who is often out of his seat. Here we are concerned with "out-of-seat" behavior. Wolf and others (1970) defined such behavior as, "the seat portion of the child's body is not in contact with any part of the seat of the child's chair." This is a clever and useful definition. Is the child displaying out-of-seat behavior if he is leaning over his desk with one knee in his chair? Yes, according to this description.

How would you describe the student who is always interrupting you? First, label the behavior you are concerned with. Here, it is "interrupting" behavior. Let's define it as "speaking to the teacher without the teacher's permission while another person is talking to the teacher or while the teacher is talking." We have to be careful that we understand the terminology even in our definitions. Also, we must be sure that other people know what we mean.

For instance, in the above definition of interrupting, just what does "permission" mean? You give permission in different ways. You might say the student's name, you might point to him, or you might merely look at him with yur eyebrows raised in a questioning manner. The important thing is to kn your mind, or better yet, written in the definition, exactly what you me might add a sentence to your definition which would explain the situation that constituted "permission." Usually we don't have to be that elaborate though.

TARGET BEHAVIOR

That behavior which is labeled, specifically defined, and is the target for observation, recording and, consequently, for modification is called the *target behavior.* In a given situation you might want to choose in-seat behavior to observe, record, and modify; in-seat behavior, then, is the target behavior. In this same situation, the student is also out-of-seat at times. If you had chosen his out-of-seat behavior to observe, record, and modify, then this out-of-seat behavior would have been the target behavior.

Some target behaviors are easier to define than others. It is relatively easy to define interrupting behavior, out-of-seat behavior, or even achievement behavior, which might be defined as the number of correctly completed mathematics problems. But what about "paying attention," an often quoted behavior. We might label this as "attending" behavior. McKenzie and others (1970) defined it as "facing instructional materials, teachers, blackboard, instructional devices, or a reciting pupil, whichever is appropriate."

You might be interested in a student who daydreams or doesn't listen to instructions. These behaviors are difficult to define, as was "paying attention." Even with the definition of facing the instructional materials, we still cannot be sure that the student is in fact "paying attention" although he might be facing the teacher.

One method that might be of value in selecting a target behavior to define when we are concerned with the more difficult-to-define behavior is to think of some behavior that the student would be doing when he was *not* displaying the target behavior. What does he do when he is *not* daydreaming, or when he *is* paying attention, or when he *is* listening? In other words, look at behavior that is *incompatible* with the original behavior of concern. After all, a student cannot work mathematics problems and daydream at the same time.

Remember, we are concerning ourselves with a behavior that is a problem and that requires a change or modification. Many teachers remark that they wish Johnny would stop fighting, stop running around the room, stop cursing, stop daydreaming, stop interrupting, etc. Notice that the teacher wants Johnny to decrease the frequency of his behavior in these areas.

Behavior modification is a philosophy or technique with a positive orientation. It can be used to increase behavior as well as decrease behavior. It is unfortunate that most teachers think only of decreasing behavior rather than increasing behavior.

Here are two ways of looking at the same thing:

Decreasing behavior	*Increasing behavior*
− stop fighting	− get along with peers
− stop running around the room	− stay in his seat more often
− stop cursing	− use more acceptable angry words
− stop interrupting	− raise his hand more often

As you are attempting to define target behavior, reconsider the problem and attempt to make the target behavior such that an increase rather than a decrease of behavior is desired. This might seem like an insignificant point, but the psychological effect of increasing a positively viewed behavior would seem to be closely related to developing a more positive self-concept of the student. Furthermore, it would seem to lend support to a more positive classroom environment.

Now try your hand at defining the target behavior in the problem you described on page 3. Remember, first label it − give it a name. Then describe it in such a way that your teacher friend would agree with you when it occurred. In fact, why not ask your friend to observe the problem and describe it.

LABEL: _____

TARGET BEHAVIOR: _____

_____

_____

_____

Knowing that behavior, an overt observable event, is definable in such a way that two or more people will agree to its occurrence or non-occurrence, it can also be measured, rated, or tallied.

CHAPTER II

Measuring
Behavior

THE MAIN REASON for measuring behavior is that, since we are only human, we find it difficult to be accurate in our recall of when and how often something happened. When the teacher said that Eddie is "constantly" on-the-go, we know that she did not mean this literally. But, how often *did* she mean? It was shown that "on-the-go" behavior did NOT mean the same thing to many people. Is it also probable that "constantly" might not be completely agreed upon by many people? Measurement can be used to show accurately how often something occurred.

Almost every teacher has run into the parent during the parent conference who simply couldn't understand why the teacher was having so much trouble with Johnny at school because at home Johnny is *alway* well behaved and *never* causes any trouble. The parent reports that he is basically a shy child and couldn't possibly be interrupting you as much as you say. Sound familiar? If that teacher had kept a record of the number of times Johnny actually *did* interrupt her over the past week, she would have some "ammunition" for the conference.

Have you ever tried to convince your principal of something only to realize that you did not have any "proof" to support your argument? In one modern school which had individual furnace-type heaters for each classroom, the teacher complained that the temperature in her room was too cold for the children to be comfortable. The children were complaining to the teacher that they were cold. When the principal heard the teacher's story he merely brushed it aside, making some remark about kids complaining about everything nowadays. A graph indicating the number of complaints made daily about the temperature in the room might have been more convincing and might have resulted in positive action.

When behavior is measured, it can serve as an objective indicator of frequency. In some situations, such as a parent conference, principal conference, or even student conference, it might serve as a form of proof or evidence to support your opinions.

One mother was concerned with the excessive number of temper tantrums her own preschooler was displaying. Following the measurement of his tantrums, she realized that they were not as frequent as she felt they were and that they occurred more often in the afternoon. As a result of measuring the tantrum behavior, the mother gained information and cues regarding when they occurred (in the afternoon before naptime) and found that her perception of the situation was different than the situation really was. A similar revelation was made to the mother who felt that she was asking her son "over and over again" before he actually did his job. Tallying the number of requests indicated that she actually was not asking as many times as she thought she was.

Measuring behavior might reveal a *pattern* of behavior which in turn might offer an explanation of the problem. Measuring behavior might also reveal that your perception of the situation in which the behavior occurred is different from the actual situation.

In order to compare your perception of the situation with the actual situation, it is necessary to observe and record the target behavior. When behavior is observed and recorded as it "naturally" occurs in situations where no programmed effort is being made by the teacher to modify it, the measured results are called *baseline* data. This information serves as a base or starting point with which we can compare the measurement of future behavior. With the results graphed, we can *see* what the behavior was like *before* we began a behavior modification project (this is the baseline data) as well as *during* the project and even *after* the project. You and others will be able to see if your program was successful. You will also be able to see *how* successful and when the change began to be observed (Lovitt, 1970).

OBSERVATION OF INTERACTION

Up to this point we have been talking primarily about measurement done by the teacher. We should not overlook the situation in which observers do the measuring of behavior — student *and* teacher behavior. Such observations have indicated that teacher behavior differs with different children. Measurement of interaction between the teacher and a child can serve as objective data for program planning. In addition, the observation suggests that what a teacher *plans* and what she *does* are often different. Measurement of behavior can be used to suggest strengths and weaknesses in the plan. Consequently, appropriate alterations can be made (Gaasholt, 1970).

While it is impossible for you to be completely objective and record interaction between yourself and a student, the values of such information might illustrate to you some of the previously mentioned values that occur from your own observing of one of your students. If you are having a "problem" with a student and you cannot quite put your finger on an objective definition of the problem, then ask someone to observe the interaction between you and the problem student. The observer might be a fellow teacher, a supervisor, a teacher's aide, the school psychologist, or anyone with whom you would feel comfortable. The observation might pinpoint the interaction behavior which in turn can be used to define a target behavior of the student for you to consider in programming for behavior modification projects.

All too often, teachers have been far less than precise in their descriptions of behavior. Recall the varied definitions of Eddie's behavior. The use of observations, recording, and measuring behavior throughout a complete program of behavior modification has been viewed as a hallmark of the philosophy of behavior modification (Wolf and Risley, 1967). The philosophy strives toward a scientific methodology. "If progress is to be made in solving the pressing educational and rehabilitative problems that face us, we must proceed with an attitude of scientific inquiry and experimentation, judging successes and failures on the basis of objective data and applying procedures systematically" (Birnbrauer and others, 1970, p. 20). Measurement can assist us toward this scientific inquiry.

Let's review the value of observing, recording, and measuring behavior. The *charted* results can be used to:

1. support your opinions about a situation or behavior which should be altered.
2. reveal a pattern of behavior which might suggest ways to alter the behavior.
3. reveal discrepancies between your perception of the situation and the situation as it exists.
4. visually indicate IF your program was successful, HOW successful it was, and WHEN the significant change occurred.
5. describe interaction for purposes of pinpointing target behavior for further programming.

How Do We Go About Measuring Behavior?

Let's say that you are interested in recording the number of times Johnny interrupts you during social studies class. You have labeled the behavior as "Interrupting" and have defined it appropriately. For your purpose you are interested in knowing *how many times* the target behavior occurred during a specified time of day. It would be nice to have the information for all day long, but this would be impractical, so we limit our recording to the forty-five minutes of social studies. Choose a time when you are able to observe every time the behavior occurs. For instance, it might be impossible to teach a reading group *and* keep track of Johnny who sits on the other side of the room.

You must record the behavior WITHOUT JOHNNY'S KNOWING THAT YOU ARE DOING SO. We'll learn why later.

There are devices available to assist in tallying behavior. Some teachers use golf-type counters that can be concealed in the palm of your hand. There are other counters that can be strapped to your wrist like a watch. It is important to point out again that the method used to count should be unnoticed by the student. Probably the slyest and most simple way is to make slash marks on a piece of paper you have tucked in your text for every time the target behavior occurs.

You want to transform the slash marks into data on a graph. The value of a visual display of your measurement cannot be understated. A graph is an easily understood format on which a great deal of information can be displayed. It is a type of summary of behavior which occurred over a period of time that can be seen at a glance, and it seems to have a greater impact than a mere column of numbers.

Your observations of Johnny during social studies might be graphed to look something like this:

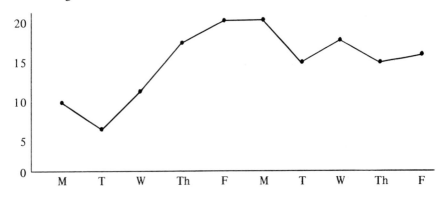

You recorded Johnny's interrupting behavior in social studies for two weeks.

You found that he interrupted you ten times on Monday, seven times on Tuesday, thirteen times on Wednesday, etc.

Suppose you wanted to record the number of times Susie went to the pencil sharpener during the math lesson. Math is taught for forty-five minutes in the morning and for forty-five minutes in the afternoon. A week's graph might look like this:

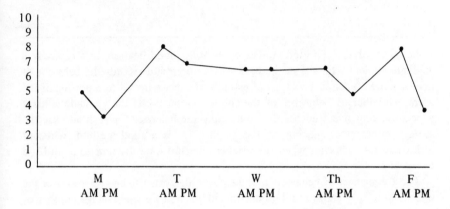

Graphs can be quite revealing or at least raise questions. For instance, why does Susie go to the pencil sharpener more often in the morning than in the afternoon? Here we have a record of the *frequency* of her visits.

Let's make a graph.

Choose any easily observed behavior to record. If you are reading this book in your teachers' or students' lounge, slyly choose someone to observe. Since your coffee break or free period probably doesn't last too long, choose some short-term behavior. A choice might be the number of bites used to consume a doughnut. You might tally the number of complete and incomplete sentences each person spoke in a conversation as you eavesdrop. If you are reading at home, you might tally the number of times someone changes position or crosses his feet while watching a TV show. Possibly you might tally the number of puffs on a cigarette for each cigarette smoked during a TV show. You might observe the number of sips taken from a cup of coffee, etc. If you are a student in a class, you might observe your professor, another student, or even yourself. Most people have some habitual behavior that can easily be recorded in a fairly short period of time. Place your information below:

LABEL: _____

DESCRIPTION: _____

_____

GRAPH

In many of the reported studies on behavior modification, it is typically a graduate student who sits in the back of the room and records the behavior of one or more students. This type of recording lends itself well to reporting of the average number of behaviors of the children observed. If the graduate student were observing five students, he could tally the behavior for each and use the average number for placing on the graph. This is a good method to record high-frequency behavior when the teacher does not have the time to record and to teach.

The frequencies of behaviors that were recorded can also be averaged over the week and a new graph can be constructed to indicate the average number of behaviors per week.

If you ever need to have two or more students observed simultaneously, it is practically impossible for you to record their behavior and teach at the same time. Ask a fellow teacher to help you out or train an aide or parent to assist you.

You might be interested in recording how long a student spends actually working on his problems during a given amount of study time. This is easy to record with a stop watch. Start the watch when he begins to work and stop it when he stops working. Let the watch run only when he is actually working. In a study period time of fifteen minutes, record the cumulative time he spent working. The graph might look like this:

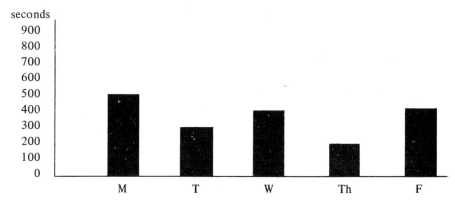

All of the above graphs present the RATE of behavior. They are simply raw counts of frequency. They indicate the frequency of events per unit of time. The other method of measurement is the RATIO method which tells what actually happened divided by what might have happened (Lovitt, 1970).

There are times when the ratio type of recording is necessary. Let's say that you are going to observe the amount of time Johnny stays out of his seat for any reason. Because of your schedule, you cannot set aside a prespecified amount of time each day to observe. Therefore, for each day you must record the out-of-seat behavior *in addition* to the amount of time you spend in observing.

Let's say you made the following chart:

	Number of minutes Bill was out of his seat	Length of time observed	Percentage of out-of-seat behavior
Monday	8	20 minutes	40%
Tuesday	2	5 minutes	40%
Wednesday	4	10 minutes	40%
Thursday	5	15 minutes	33%
Friday	6	12 minutes	50%

Using the above you will want to make a graph:

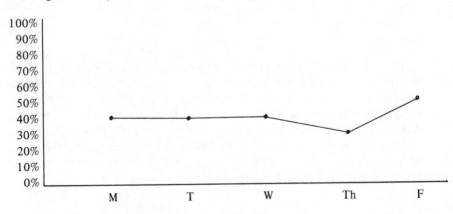

The information indicates that Bill was out of his seat about 40 percent of the time — at least about 40 percent of the time the teacher was observing him.

Try your hand at making a ratio graph. A stop watch is helpful, but if you do not have one, try this: Choose a time during the school day just prior to when a bell is rung. This will signal the end of your observation period. Bells usually ring to signal the beginning of home room, end of recess, change of classes, etc. Choose a varying number of minutes before the bell to begin your observation. For instance, to observe how long Susie keeps the pencil in her mouth, you might choose five minutes before the homeroom bell, the last ten minutes before recess, and three minutes before the bell to change classes, etc. As you watch

Susie, say to yourself, "one thousand . . . two thousand . . . three thousand . . . etc." to approximate the passage of time in seconds. You would count the seconds only when the behavior was being exhibited. Total the number of seconds you observed the behavior and record it in addition to the amount of time you spent observing. Actually, any method of keeping an accurate record of time is perfectly acceptable.

After you have recorded the necessary information, compute the percentages and graph your results here:

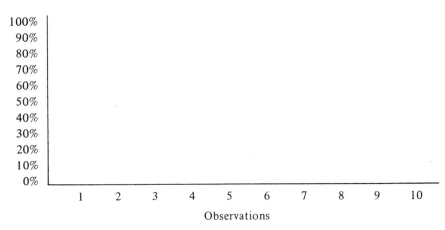

If you could get a friend to do some observing for you, another method is to observe at prespecified time intervals. In a thirty minute lesson the student is observed for ten seconds every three minutes. There will be ten observations made within the lesson. Of course the behavior to be observed is labeled and well defined before the observation is made. For the series of observations, the observer might merely record a "+" if the student is doing some preestablished and defined behavior or a "−" if the student is not doing it. An example might be "staring-out-of-the-window" behavior. Your record might show:

	Frequency of +	Number of Observations	Percent
Monday	1	10	10%
Tuesday	0	10	0%
Wednesday	5	10	50%
Thursday	3	10	30%
Friday	4	10	40%

This chart illustrates the percentage of time that the student was observed staring out of the window. It suggests that possibly an interesting lesson was presented at the first part of the week and an exceptionally boring lesson was given on Wednesday.

If you have not had a chance to observe a student to gather the information to make a graph, refer to the case study and chart the information the teacher recorded about Charlie's correct answers to his math papers. Use the graph below:

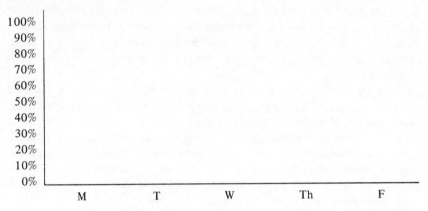

Of all the methods of recording behavior that have been discussed, the easiest method for teachers is the simple tallying of the frequency of the target behavior. This is easily done in a book that the teacher carries around. The information is then transferred to a graph to visually illustrate the frequency of the target behavior.

TAKING THE BIG STEP

You have learned how to label and describe the target behavior that you feel deserves to be modified. Also, you have learned about several methods of recording and graphing the results of your observations. The method you choose actually depends upon the behavior and the circumstances under which it can be observed.

Now your task is to begin observing and recording the target behavior you have labeled and described. You should do this for a least a week to establish some reliable data. Probably a two-week period might even give you a better indication of the stability of the student's behavior. Remember that this information will be the baseline data.

You will be surprised at the information that you obtain merely during the process of purposeful observation. Also, you will be suprised at the picture of your observations you will have after they are graphed. If you are not surprised, you will at least be pleased at the visible effort of the work you have done.

During the next two-week period you will spend most of your time observing the student. It will be a good idea to begin observing him not only for the target behavior but for other behaviors as well. You should take a few minutes to jot down any special events that occur each day. Watch what the student does *before* he displays the target behavior and watch what he does *after* he displays it. Watch also for the events in the surrounding environment that are taking place before, during, and after the target behavior occurs. Watch what the student does in his spare time; watch what he does when he should be doing an assigned lesson. What are his own choices of behaviors? Jot down this information.

Since for the next few days, your only task is simple observation, you should continue reading the next chapter of this book which will explain the theory, background, and certain points of special interest to educators. It is important to become quite knowledgeable with the theory. At first, it seems quite simple — almost pure common sense, then it becomes an ever increasingly complex interplay of necessary behaviors on the part of the person who is managing the environment in order to modify the behavior of the student. Usually the person with this responsibility is you, the teacher.

Whenever a teacher remarks that whatever he tried did not work, the reasons for its not working can usually be traced to the particular program that the teacher arranged, not to the theory. With a good grasp of the theory, the chances are better that you will be able to establish a correct and more positive program for modification of behavior.

It is important over the next two weeks, while you are obtaining the base-line data, that you actively avoid any attempts at purposeful changes for modifying the student's behavior. The real purpose of the baseline observations is to obtain a picture of the target behavior PRIOR to any planned program for change.

CHAPTER **III**

Understanding
Behavior

"THEORY IS A bunch of bunk!"

"Those college profs — all they do is talk about theory, theory, theory! Yet, they never tell us what to do with it."

"Throw theory out the window. Let's see some action!"

Shades of the teacher's lounge? Probably. Some teachers typically are turned off by theory — at least that is what they complain about while taking college classes. Yet, when they are asked to explain the reading program, their use of theory becomes apparent in that they follow a developmental sequence rather rigidly. When asked why they might do this, they respond with, "Well, we teach short vowels first because the theory of reading states that they are easier to learn."

"Why are you using this modern math text?"

"It helps the kids to understand the meaning of math."

"How do you know?"

"Well, theoretically, it makes sense."

It seems that while teachers complain about theory, they still refer to it as providing a guideline within which they actually do fit the practicalities of instruction.

Students and practicing teachers have expressed dissatisfaction with the lack of instruction on how to apply theory to practical situations. "While teachers usually are required to take numerous psychology courses, most of these deal with broad principles, theoretical constructs, and rather general statements about children, learning, and teaching. The teacher is left with the burden of fitting this information into the scheme of his specific class. This usually is not only difficult, but also can lead to misintrepretation and imprecision. Few branches of psychology have made attempts to bridge this gap, but with the recent inception of behavior modification techniques the attempt has begun" (Whitman and Whitman, 1971, p. 177).*

In our quest for techniques and methodologies to deal with the behavior of students who are problems in the classroom, we began (in the first two chapters) by being quite specific and objective. You might say that we are approaching this job from a scientific angle.

Kerlinger discusses theory as one of the basic aims of science. "This discussion of the basic aim of science as theory may seem strange to the student, especially the student of education, who has probably been inculcated with the notion that human activities have to pay off in practical ways. If we said that the aim of science is the betterment of mankind most readers would quickly read the words and accept them. But the basic aim of science is not the betterment of mankind. It is theory. Unfortunately, this sweeping and really complex statement is not too easy to understand. Still, we must try because it is important" (1965, pp. 10-11).

Kerlinger defines theory as "a set of interrelated constructs (concepts), definitions, and propositions that present a systematic view of phenomena by specifying relations among variables, with the purpose of explaining and predicting the phenomena" (1965, p. 11).

THE THEORY OF BEHAVIOR MODIFICATION

If our task is to know how to deal with students' behavior, we must be able to explain a student's behavior and to predict, from that explanation, how the student is likely to act in the future. In other words, we need a theory to help us do this.

In this chapter we will learn such a theory. A thorough knowledge of the theory is necessary in order for us to be able to decide how we as teachers are to behave when we are dealing with the target student.

*The material quoted here and elsewhere in this book from Myron Whitman and Joan Whitman, "Behavior Modification in the Classroom," *Psychology in the Schools,* 1971, pp. 176-186, reprinted by permission of Clinical Psychology Publishing Company and the authors.

We will learn about the learning theory of reinforcement. When the principles of this theory are used in dealing with humans, we usually speak of this as "behavior modification." Behavior modification is the application of knowledge from experimental psychology with animals applied to humans and mixed with a lot of scientifically stated common sense (Poteet, 1970). Whitman and Whitman (1971) define it as "the use of learning theory principles to alter maladaptive behavior. These principles have evolved out of many years of research with humans and animals; the systematic application of these principles to maladaptive behavior patterns is behavior modification."

Behavior modification is seen by Chaffin and Kroth (1971) as the management of behavior through the manipulation of the environment. Gelfand and Hartmann (1968), in discussing behavior therapy, a corollary of behavior modification, define it as "treatment techniques derived from theories of learning and aimed at the direct modification of one or more problem behaviors rather than at effecting more general and less observable personality or adjustment changes" (p. 205).

Notice that they mention the lack of emphasis on "less observable personality or adjustment changes." Kerlinger discussed a similar concern that scientists have about prediction. "It is obvious that explanation and prediction can be subsumed under theory. The very nature of a theory lies in its explanation of observed phenomena. Take reinforcement theory in psychology. A simple proposition flowing from this theory is: If a response is rewarded (reinforced) when it occurs, it will tend to be repeated. The psychological scientist who first formulated some such proposition did so as an explanation of the observed repetitious occurrences of responses. *Why* did they occur and reoccur with dependable regularity? Because they were rewarded ... If by using the theory we are able to predict successfully, then the theory is confirmed and this is enough. We need not necessarily look for further underlying explanations" (1965, p. 11-12).

Remember back in the first chapter, you were concerned with objectively labeling and defining behavior. You also listed what in your opinion *caused* the problem. What other teachers thought were causes was also discussed. Many of their causes seemed to lie somewhere "within" the student (i.e., emotional problem, certain needs, low ability, attitude toward parents, etc.). It is almost as if the behavior in the classroom were considered a "symptom" of these underlying "causes"; consequently, the "causes" are analogous to a disease which must be "cured" before the symptoms disappear.

Have you ever thought to yourself, "I don't know how I can be expected to teach *that* kid with all the hurt and anger he has inside him. I think he's emotionally disturbed. He needs a psychiatrist – I can't do anything for him!" If you have thought along these lines, you were probably thinking that the student needed a therapist to "cure" the "disease" of emotional disturbance so you could get down to the business of teaching. You were, inadvertently, assuming that the approach that medical doctors use to cure pneumonia would work with your student. This medical approach to curing illnesses is typically called "the medical model."

Stuart discussed several reasons why the medical model is sometimes used in the study of behavior.

This model assumes that an apparent problem of human behavior is a symptom of an underlying pathogenic condition in much the same way that elevations of fever or white corpuscle count are manifestations of infection in the body. To continue the argument, it is assumed that unless the pathogen is removed, a greater number of possibly more severe symptomatic problems will result.

This model has obviously worked well in the treatment of physical ailments, and this success is perhaps the chief reason for the willingness of psychotherapists to accept the approach. A second reason may be the simplicity of the model with its appeal of parsimony. A third reason might be the emotional appeal of the argument (Scheflen, 1958), which carries with it an implicit guarantee that once the pathogen has been named it can be removed, resulting in cure.

In order for the model to be legitimately applied to psychotherapy, it must be shown to be appropriate and useful. There is good reason to believe that it is neither . . . Beyond arguments about the legitimacy of the metaphor drawn between the medical model and psychotherapy, one can also argue that there is voluminous data to support the view that the medical model is not useful and must be purged from our scientific approaches to behavior change (1970, pp. 6-8).

Stuart (1970) devoted an entire book to the review of research to support his statements mentioned above. In the foreword to this book, Wolpe stated that:

Psychoanalytic theory, which has dominated psychiatric thinking for half a century, attributes the symptoms of "functional" psychiatric illness to hidden internal sources. The existence of these hidden processes has never been demonstrated. Nevertheless, the psychoanalytically oriented therapist assumes their presence in every case and then purports to derive a detailed image of them from the patient's verbalizations. This is not difficult to do, and rewarded by the approval of colleagues, soon becomes a confident habit. Dr. Stuart shows how conclusions drawn from these ratiocinations not only fail to bear therapeutic fruit, but often actually hurt the patient. Besides the direct harm that wrong treatment can do, indirect damage can be done by pejorative inferences that may be conveyed quite blatantly or by innuendos borne on such phrases as "may be significant" (1970).

The approach taken by some therapists is explained by Whitman and Whitman:

Most psychotherapies have followed the assumptions of the medical model. Clients are viewed as having certain psychological symptoms –

maladaptive or inappropriate behaviors, beliefs or attitudes. The therapist attempts to discover and to treat the underlying psychological disturbance that causes the symptoms. The underlying disturbance that is treated varies according to the theoretical orientation of the therapist and the particular client involved. Removal or healing of the underlying disturbance should, according to the dictates of the medical model, be accompanied by symptom alleviation . . . In this model [the behavioral model] the more overt and obvious psychological problems of the client (symptoms) are treated directly. There is no attempt to postulate and treat underlying psychological illnesses. The symptoms are the illness (1971, p. 178).

But how can you explain the situation in which you think one set of behaviors has been "cured," only to find a new set of behaviors appear that are almost as detrimental; isn't that simply more "symptoms" coming out because the "real" reason was not dealt with? This is a typical question raised by skeptics of the behavioral learning theory. When this situation occurs within the medical model, it is referred to as symptom substitution; one symptom is substituted for another when the treatment is aimed only at the symptom, while the disease has not been treated. This is true of medicine but not in the behavioral sciences. Whitman and Whitmen cite research indicating little or no empirical evidence for symptom substitution. They point out that:

... evidence exists, however, to show that improvement in one maladaptive behavior tends to generalize to other maladaptive behaviors (Lang, 1969); this positive generalization is opposite to that which would be predicted by the symptom substitution hypothesis. If, however, other maladaptive behaviors did replace the treated and "cured" symptomatic behavior, explanations exist that are more compelling than that of symptom substitution. For instance, if behavior is extinguished (i.e., ceases to be reinforced or rewarded and therefore ceases to occur), it is likely that the behavior with the next highest probability of being emitted in that situation is also a maladaptive behavior. In this example, one maladaptive behavior replaced another, but it was not necessary to postulate an underlying illness as the cause of this substitution" (1971, p. 178).

Krasner and Ullmann (1965) cited research which indicates that evidence for symptom substitution is slight; they offer an explanation which renders it highly untenable. Stuart (1970) also cited evidence which indicated that it was not demonstrated, that the validity of the analogy to the medical model is questionable, and that sometimes the approach is unsuccessful. Meacham (1968) noted that behavior modification has been effective for many kinds of disorders (phobias, anxiety reactions, enuresis, stuttering, and tics) and that the modified behaviors were long lasting, with no evidence of symptom substitution.

Relating the medical model to learning, Mowrer pointed out that:

There is no way in which the concept of disease or illness can be expressed in terms of learning theory. The principles, or "laws," of learn-

ing presuppose a normally functioning nervous system. And the mechanisms thus identified either work out well for a given organism, or badly,
according to the nature of the circumstances and the adequacy of these
mechanisms. In other words, the native and acquired means of coping with
a given situation that a specific organism has may or may not result in
adjustment and integration, but the failure of these means is better
described as limitation, stupidity, or incompetence than as sickness. There
is thus literally no way of talking about illness in the vocabulary of learning theory. Just as some societies are said to have no word for a particular
phenomenon or concept, so it may be said that those who use the language
of learning theory in a technical sense "have no word" for, or way of
conceptualizing, disease in the literal, physical sense of that term . . .

In other words, it may be said that the language of learning theory and
the language of disease and its treatment (medicine) are incommensurate.
They are two different "universes of discourse," and only confusion can
result when they are indiscriminately mixed (1969, p. 538).

Arthur cited evidence to support his objection to the concept of mental
illness which he feels presents several other approaches to solving the problem of
concern. "The most influential alternative approach is that many psychological
disturbances are aspects of learning" (Arthur, 1969, p. 185).

Rather than some unseen underlying cause being contributory to behavior,
Krasner and Ullmann (1965) emphasize the effect of environmental stimulation
in directing the individual's behavior. They virtually eliminate hypothetical concepts such as the unconscious, ego, and internal dynamics. Heredity and maturation are also de-emphasized. Their approach to maladaptive behavior is through a
psychological rather than a medical model, and the psychological model is social
reinforcement. Other human beings are a source of meaningful stimuli that alter,
direct, or maintain the individual's behavior.

In summarizing Ferster's chapter in their book, Krasner and Ullmann point
out that he "argues that environmental stimuli, rather than underlying illness or
intrapsychic conflict, determine and maintain what is labeled as deviant, maladaptive, inappropriate, disadvantageous, or disruptive behavior. The ab-
normality is not a problem within the individual that must be rationalized by
recourse to concepts such as repression, displacement, or symbolization, but
rather is the result of the person's interaction with his social environment and
represents an understandable outcome of the individual's history of reinforcement" (1965, p. 6).

Environmental forces are an integral part of behavior modification which
adopts the *behavioral* model rather than the medical model discussed above. In
his discussion of the behavior model as a new alternative approach to diagnosis,
Arthur stated that:

The origin of this approach is in the behavioristic psychology of Pavlov,
Watson, Dunlap, Hull, and Skinner. Its application to the problems of

diagnosis and assessment is recent and mainly associated with behavior modification techniques ... For Krumboltz (1966), the advantages of the learning approach to behavior problems lie in the principles that there is much evidence and knowledge on the problems of learning, ánd learning is integrated with the enterprise of modification, that the goals of learning can be defined and reached better than those of other techniques, that learning focuses more on action than on problems, and that patients can be expected to face an increased sense of responsibility for their actions when they become aware that they can learn effective ways of dealing with their problems (1969, p. 187-188).

In describing the approach therapists take within the behavioral model, Whitman and Whitman discuss the futility of labeling a person according to the concepts found in the medical model.

The behavior therapist believes that all behavior — adaptive and mal-adaptive, appropriate and inappropriate — is learned and maintained according to the same principles. The concept of abnormal, diseased, or "sick" is not included in this model, since all behavior is believed to be acquired, continued or discontinued in a like manner. There appear to be, however, some behaviors that are more acceptable or rewarding to the individual or to his particular society and which therefore are labeled "normal." To label certain other behaviors "sick" seems to imply a psychological discontinuity between these and "normal" behaviors. In reality, "sick" behaviors seem to be those behaviors that are not accept-able to the individual or to his society. "Sick" and "normal" behavior vary markedly across cultures. The societal determination of the acceptability of specific behaviors is exemplified by the witch doctor. This very esteemed and respected member of certain societies very probably would be confined to a mental institution in twentieth-century America due to his hallucinations, bizarre thinking, and lack of contact with reality (1971, p. 179-180).

"Behavior therapy differs from traditional psychotherapy in that it starts from the premise that psychological disorders represent learned behavior and that known principles of learning can be applied to their modification" (Ross, 1967). Instead of the disorder being symptomatic of some underlying disease which must be cured, the behavior therapist deals with the manifest behavior, feeling that while antecedent events might be related, it is not necessary to reconstruct the past to change the behavior (Ross, 1967).

By now you should have a pretty good idea of what the medical model is and how the learning theory of reinforcement in behavior modification differs from it. The reasons for the difference will become more clear as you learn more about the theory.

If it now seems that all of the talk about behavior *therapy* and *treatment* just does not apply to the instructional process in the classroom, then try substi-tuting "teaching" for "behavior therapy" and "instruction" for "treatment."

jou and Baer (1961) incorporate the concepts of behavior psychology in their natural science approach to child behavior and development. They are interested only in observable, recordable instances of responses of the developing child. They state that behavior (B) is a function (f) of, or is a consequence of, stimulus events (S). Therefore, B = f(S). Stimulus events can be physical, chemical, biological, or social — any or all of which act on the individual. Any interaction between the stimulus and the response is a unified response system in relation to the environment — a part of which might be the body. Behavior can be caused physically, such as a pain in the stomach, or socially, such as telephoning the doctor. Most of the conditions determining psychological behavior, however, are social, with the influences beginning at birth and continuing throughout the life span.

Other social beings make demands: "Brush your teeth in the morning"; set occasions for behavior: "It's time for lunch"; approve behavior: "Atta boy!"; punish and disapprove: "Go to the principal's office"; bring non-social pain: "Open up so the dentist can drill your tooth"; signify socially approved actions: "Put your napkin on your lap"; and set the level of skill: "If your work has more than one spelling error, you will flunk" (Bijou and Baer, 1961).

Up to this point we have been comparing the medical model and the behavior learning model of reinforcement used in the study of behavior modification. We also looked at a child development point of view. With this background, it is time we plunged into the nitty gritty of terminology of the theory. It is the terminology that allows us to communicate and to realize the meaning of the theory.

RESPONDENT AND OPERANT BEHAVIOR

There are two broad classifications of behavior which evolved from the work of Pavlov, Watson, Thorndike, Skinner, Hull and others — namely respondent and operant behavior.

Respondent behavior (also called reflex behavior) is that behavior in which responses are strengthened or weakened primarily by stimuli that precede the response. A typical example is the reduction in the size of the pupil of the eye when a bright light is presented. The bright light (stimulus) preceded the reduction in the size of the pupil (response). The startle reflex is another example. When you sneak up behind someone and burst a paper bag full of air (stimulus), the person jumps (response). The reason this behavior is called reflex behavior is obvious; the response is made quickly, without "thinking" — reflexively. Although these types of responses are called reflexes, some people think that even they can be conditioned so that, even with a bright light shining in your eyes, you can still keep the pupil dilated. This occurs after some amount of "training," however.

Operant behavior is the other broad classification of behavior. The individual "operates" upon his environment to produce a certain event. The student raises his hand (operates upon his environment) and the teacher calls on him (produces an event). Remember that respondent (reflexive) behavior occurs practically automatically when certain special stimuli are presented. But in operant behavior there might be times when there are no specific stimuli available to evoke certain responses. We then are compelled to wait until they appear before we can respond. Teachers sometimes have to use ingenious techniques in order to get a student to do something (operate upon his environment) before she can respond (the event he wanted to produce) (Keller, 1954).

When behavior is manipulated, the term "conditioning" is used. In respondent conditioning a goal might be to obtain a new stimulus that will elicit the reflexive behavior. For example, Keller (1954) reported an experiment in which a subject puts his right hand in cold water and the temperature of his left hand drops automatically. A buzzer is sounded just before the right hand is repeatedly placed in the cold water. By the twentieth time this was done (paired), the buzzer alone would elicit the temperature change in the left hand. This experiment indicated that a neutral stimulus (the buzzer) when paired or presented just before the eliciting stimulus (cold water) will come to elicit the same response. Timing is important here; if there had been a delay in time between the buzzer and the cold water, conditioning would not have occurred. A stimulus (the buzzer) which is *not* part of the reflex relationship became the *conditioned* stimulus for the response (temperature drop in the left hand) by repeated temporal pairing with an *unconditioned* stimulus (the cold water) which already elicited the response. This new relationship is called a conditioned reflex, and that pairing procedure is called respondent conditioning (Michael and Meyerson, 1966). This type of conditioning is not permanent unless the relationship is maintained.

Operant conditioning, on the other hand, is described by Thorndike's "Law of Effect" which states that an act may be altered in its strength by its consequence. The consequence of operant behavior is called a reinforcer. Therefore, a reinforcer is something that "controls" (strengthens or weakens, increases or decreases) some act (behavior). We will talk more about reinforcers later.

The strength of the *response* is measured by how fast the response is made when the subject is free to respond (Keller, 1954) and depends upon the number of times it has been reinforced in the past (Bijou and Baer, 1961). Sometimes, however, a satiation effect is observed when the reinforcers lose their reinforcing value. When the behavior is "controlled" through such selective reinforcement, this procedure is called operant conditioning, instrumental conditioning, or effect learning.

In operant conditioning we do not produce new responses, we strengthen or weaken, increase or decrease old ones and put them together in new combinations. It is easy to see that the interest in behavior modification, especially when related to education, is primarily concerned with operant conditioning.

A *stimulus* is something that acts on the individual. The child possesses within himself the capacity to produce stimuli that can affect his behavior just as stimuli originating from the external environment affect his behavior. He can feel pressure from the bladder, remind himself that it is time to leave a party, change his method of pedaling a bicycle, etc. The behavior of the child provides social stimuli to other people (Bijou and Baer, 1961), maybe even to teachers.

A *positive reinforcer* is synonymous with a reward. It strengthens or increases the desired behavior. It must be given immediately after the response occurs. This probably is the single most important principle of operant conditioning (Watson), and consequently of behavior modification.

Premack observed that reinforcement involves a relation typically between two responses, one that is being reinforced and another that is responsible for the reinforcement. This leads to the generalization that "of any two responses, the more probable response will reinforce the less probable one" (1965, p. 132). This generalization has become known as the "Premack Principle," and it has been used in many studies as a theoretical base. In a booklet to explain the principles of behavior modification to parents, Becker (1971) refers to this as "Grandma's Rule." This rule is expressed in such comments as: "You can play ball when you finish your homework," or "You can go out and play after you take out the trash." It is summarized as first you work, then you play. The more probable response, playing, reinforces the less probable one, working. Therefore, the reward for working is playing.

In the example involving putting a hand in cold water, we learned that the buzzer became the conditioned stimulus. Reinforcers also can be "conditioned" to become meaningful. When a smile is paired with a candy bar, the smile soon becomes the only reinforcer necessary. In other words, it becomes a *secondary* reinforcer. The candy bar was the *primary* reinforcer. You can understand why this is important to know, especially when we apply this theory to teaching. We cannot go around handing out candy bars, M & Ms, raisins, or what have you all of the time. Not only does it become expensive, usually to the teacher, but the parents and the students might soon tire of these reinforcers. In education, reinforcers are socially approved rewards for behavior such as smiles, a pat on the back, positive verbalization, check marks, etc.

Some of you are probably thinking "OK. I can see that a candy bar might be used as a primary reinforcer to get a kid going on some behavior. *But,* what about the *other* kids who see Johnny getting a candy bar? Won't they also want a candy bar for doing the same thing?"

They might. But teachers are typically rather autocratic. Susie asks if she can wash the chalkboard. You respond, "No! Sit down." Susie sits down and doesn't think too much more about it. Teachers also can say, "No. This candy bar is for Johnny because he earned it," or some such remark. Usually the student will accept a factual remark of this sort (Kroth, 1970).

If you are a more non-autocratic type, you might go into more detail explaining why the candy bar was given. You might even use candy bars as reinforcers for the students who asked in order to modify their behavior. It obviously is a reinforcer for them or they probably wouldn't have asked. Children often model after the teacher. If she is happy that Johnny received a reward, usually the other children are happy that Johnny received a reward.

POSITIVE AND NEGATIVE REINFORCERS

There are two types of reinforcers: positive and negative. When positive reinforcers are presented, the behavior that was occurring prior to use of the positive reinforcer increases or is maintained. When negative reinforcers are presented, the behavior that was occurring prior to use of the negative reinforcer decreases or terminates.

Johnny was sitting quietly in his seat reading, the teacher gave him some sort of positive reinforcer, and he continued to read quietly. Susie was talking to herself and not reading, the teacher did something, such as tap sharply on the desk which served as a negative reinforcer, and she quit talking to herself and became quiet.

Positive Reinforcer → increased behavior
(being quiet)

Negative Reinforcer → decreased behavior
(talking)

The converse of the situation is also true. "A positive reinforcer . . . decreases the probability of the response that removes it, and a negative reinforcer . . . increases the probability of the response that removes it" (Holgate, 1971, p. 3).

Negative reinforcers might need to be clarified. Generally a reinforcer is defined as a stimulus which *increases* the rate of behavior. When a positive reinforcer is presented, the rate of behavior prior to the reinforcer tends to increase. This is rather easy to understand. The trick comes when we discuss negative reinforcers. How can a negative reinforcer *increase* the rate of behavior? After all, we did say that reinforcers were defined as stimuli which *increase* behavior.

The rate of behavior increases when the negative reinforcer is *removed;* the rate of behavior increases when a positive reinforcer is *given*. Therein lies the difference.

The idea of "removing" reinforcers seems strange to teachers, especially since we beat our brains out trying to find reinforcers to give. The problem is that we typically think of a reinforcer as a "good"thing, so we want to reward a student for good behavior. The negative reinforcer is the other side of the coin. Negative reinforcers "are those stimuli whose *withdrawal* reinforces behavior. Such negative reinforcers reduce the rate of responses that produce them and increase the rate of responses leading to their removal" (*Psychology Today, an Introduction*, 1970, p. 120).

The yelling that a teacher might do for students to get in their seats can be considered a negative reinforcer. When the yelling stops, the behavior that stopped it (removed it) was in-seat behavior. Therefore, in-seat behavior increases and out-of-seat behavior (which produced the yelling) is reduced.

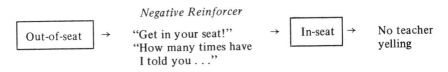

In our earlier example, the positive reinforcer would, in addition to increasing Johnny's being quiet, also decrease the probability of his talking. The negative reinforcer, in addition to decreasing Susie's talking also increases the probability of her being quiet.

Positive Reinforcer: Increases being quiet AND decreases talking
Negative Reinforcer: Decreases talking AND increases being quiet

This can generalize to a model of reinforcement:

MODEL OF REINFORCEMENT

Positive Reinforcer:	Increase A	Decrease B
Negative Reinforcer:	Decrease B	Increase A

With this model in mind, you now can see that both positive and negative reinforcers can either increase or decrease behavior; it all depends on how it's done. Think of behavior "A" and "B" as incompatible. If the student is doing "A," there would be no possibility that he could be doing "B" at the same time.

If you wanted to decrease Johnny's talking out without permission, then talking out would be labeled "B," What behavior would be incompatible with this? Raising his hand would naturally be labeled "A." Positive reinforcement would increase hand raising ("A"), while it decreased talking out ("B"). Negative reinforcement, possibly scolding, would decrease talking out ("B") and increase hand raising ("A").

Chaffin and Kroth (1971) gave the example of nagging a child to pick up his clothes. Mother's behavior, nagging, was a negative reinforcer which decreased the behavior of leaving clothes on the floor and increased the behavior of hanging his clothes up. The child decided that it would be better to hang up his clothes rather than to listen to his mother nag; he "escaped" her nagging.

In behavior modification the emphasis is upon positive reinforcement rather than on negative reinforcement. The side effects of negative reinforcement are such that other less desired behaviors become apparent. These behaviors are not conducive to positive adjustment. We will learn more about the effects of negative reinforcement later on.

What happens when we *remove* a positive reinforcer?

When *all* positive reinforcement is removed from a situation, the behavior that was receiving the reinforcement seems to terminate – it becomes extinguished. The plan of withdrawing or removing a positive reinforcer is called *extinction.* This is a common method used in behavior modification to change behavior. In the classroom, when the teacher chooses to ignore certain behaviors, the behavior stops because the student is not being reinforced for his behavior. This is another method used to decrease and eventually terminate certain behavior. The saying, "Ignore it and maybe it will go away," has more truth than fiction to it.

This approach to changing behavior is important to know because, in some cases, it is quite useful. However, even this approach has certain drawbacks. Clarizio and Yelon (1967) presented these cautions:

1. spontaneous remission or the return of undesirable behavior may occur following extinction, necessitating additional extinction,
2. peers intermittently reinforce maladaptive behavior without the complete control of the teacher, and
3. some teachers cannot afford to wait long enough for extinction to occur, especially when the possibility of emotional contagion (other students' being influenced by one student) or self-injury is evident.

PUNISHMENT

We've been talking about removing reinforcers. When a positive reinforcer is taken away *or* when a negative reinforcer is presented, we have what is known to us as *punishment.*

"There is probably no other area in the psychology of behavior where more emotion, confusion, and misunderstanding have been generated than over the topic of punishment. Teachers and parents have been told that they should not use punishment because it doesn't work. It supposedly only produces temporary effects. Some people believe that any use of punishment under any circumstances is immoral. Some people believe it is all right to punish children severely as long as you don't slap them in the face. Some equate any form of isolation procedure with prison, failing to be concerned with the benefits to the child. Some believe we should ban the word from the English language, as if that would somehow make people more loving" (Becker, 1971, p. 121).*

Punishment is an intervention technique which has been used to discourage or to decrease certain undesirable behavior. Usually it occurs in the form of presentation of a negative reinforcer which typically represents either physically painful stimuli (spanking) or psychologically painful stimuli (embarrassment) when the undesirable behavior occurs.

Remember when we remarked that we would discuss the effects that occur when negative reinforcers were presented? Now we can see that we were talking about the undesirable effects that occur when punishment is used. Clarizio and Yelon (1967) have set forth some reasons for not using punishment, viewed as presenting a negative reinforcer:

1. it does not eliminate, it merely slows down the behavior,
2. it does not show what appropriate behavior is,
3. aggressive behavior on the teacher's part during punishment may serve as an inappropriate model for the child,
4. the emotional results such as fear, tenseness, and withdrawal are maladaptive, and
5. it serves as a source of frustrations which lead to more maladaptive behavior.

They point out that punishment allows undesirable behavior to be held in abeyance, thus permitting the teaching of desirable modes of behavior through social imitation and positive reinforcement.

Punishment does cause a quick decrease in the target behavior. A more gradual decrease in the target behavior could have been obtained through the procedure of extinction. Extinction procedures are more effective than punishment when there is a continuation of non-reinforcement because when punishment is discontinued, the original behavior that you wanted to decrease or stop simply returns; if non-reinforcement is continued through the process of extinction, the target behavior remains extinguished. Extinction, non-reinforcement, probably cannot be truly considered as punishment.

Suppose that as a teacher you used punishment, the presentation of a negative reinforcer, to eliminate out-of-seat behavior. It works and it works quickly as long as you continue to use it. Then one day you are absent from school and a substitute teacher takes over your class. She reports to you the next day when you return that Johnny certainly was out of his seat more than he should have

*The material quoted here and elsewhere in this book from Wesley Becker, *Parents are Teachers: A Child Management Program,* Champaign, Ill.: Research Press Company, reprinted with permission.

been. His behavior returned because the substitute teacher did not use punishment to decrease the target behavior as you had continuously done.

Punishment does result in certain effects that are undesirable. There is active learning to avoid or to escape from the punishing situation. The student might still want to get out of his seat; the desire remains at the same level of persistence, but it is overcome only for the moment in order to *avoid* the punishment situation which would occur if he did get out of his seat. This distinction is of practical significance in the control of behavior (Berelson and Steiner, 1964).

Becker, Thomas, and Carnine (1969) in their review of principles of operant conditioning for teachers give a good summary of the effects and use of punishment. They reported studies showing that criticism, instead of being a punisher, merely positively reinforced misbehavior. Quiet reprimands were more effective than loud reprimands during a rest period. They indicated that while punishment can be very effective in controlling behavior, it should be used in only those few cases that occur frequently and intently where there is fear of danger to the child or to others.

Two important things are learned by the student when he is punished. He learns to avoid or to escape from the person doing the punishing. If the feelings of avoidance and escape are directed against teachers, there then is a loss of control that the teacher has over learning. "Avoidance and escape behavior often have names such as lying, hiding, truancy, cheating on exams, doing things behind one's back, etc. Accompanying such avoidance and escape behaviors are negative feelings for the persons who use punishment. For the most part, the teacher is wise to find other means for influencing children" (Becker, Thomas, and Carnine, 1969).

The student:

increases:	in-seat
decreases:	out-of-seat
learns:	to avoid the wrath of the teacher
feels:	punished

Negative Reinforcer

Out-of-Seat	$\rightarrow$ "Get in your seat! I've told you a thousand times . . ."	$\uparrow$ In-Seat

Needless to say, the student in the situation above develops negative feelings for the teacher. If this is a frequent occurrence, he soon develops negative feelings toward himself and senses himself as not worthwhile.

Remember we said that punishment can also be defined as the removal of positive reinforcement? When the teacher arranges the classroom situation so that the student has time out from positive reinforcement, we have a form of punishment. In the study of behavior modification, this is an acceptable form of punishment to use. It is called the "time-out" technique. It is in effect isolation.

You probably have used it many times but maybe not in the exact way that it should be used within the framework of behavior modification. Time-out is not merely isolation. It is "time-out" from positive reinforcement. Unless there has been an ongoing classroom situation in which positive reinforcement is available on a rather continuing basis, removing a child from the classroom is in effect isolation rather than time-out from positive reinforcement. There is that subtle, but most important, difference.

Usually, in the study of behavior modification, there is a small room or a cubicle called the time-out room. The student is placed there for only a few minutes (two to five) in order not to be positively reinforced within the class-room. The reinforcement which the time-out technique seeks to avoid usually comes from peers in situations of gross overt behavior or loud verbalizations. This technique is used as a last resort in situations where the student's behavior is being positively reinforced by peers or when there is danger either to the target student, to other students, or to the teacher. It is probably surprising for you to learn of the short amount of time recommended for the student to be placed in the time-out room. Many teachers have students isolated from the classroom for hours at a time. It seems however, that the mere process of removal from positive reinforcement is enough to be effective. Therefore, re-maining in a non-positive reinforcing environment, the time-out room, for an exceedingly long amount of time is useless.

It is very important here to realize that the time-out room *must* be a situation or place in which there is absolutely *no* positive reinforcement. Many times it is actually fun to sit out in the hall or to go to the principal's office. There the student can watch everything that is going on and even sometimes help the secretary. If these situations provide any type of positive reinforcement at all, then the classroom behavior that occurred, which caused the teacher to send the student to the hall or to the principal's office, is in fact positively reinforced and will undoubtedly occur again. The teacher might then remark, "I don't know why Johnny acts up so often in class. I have to send him to the principal's office every day." It is obvious that there is more positive reinforcement for Johnny in the principal's office than in the classroom. The way out of this situation is available if the teacher would refer to the model of reinforcement presented previously. She might give consideration to positively reinforcing behavior in-compatible to the behavior that she negatively reinforced or punished.

Some of you might find it unusual to think of punishment in the broad sense we have used here. Usually we think of punishment only as a spanking, a hit, a slap, or some such act. But, recall that many people also say that they "punish" their child by "taking away privileges" – a form of removal of positive rein-forcer.

Punishment, in this broad definition, operates to various degrees. For in-stance, finger snapping by the teacher to stop whispering can be considered as a presentation of a negative reinforcer and consequently a very mild form of "punishment." While some of you might disagree that finger snapping is, in fact, punishment, you would all agree that a spanking is punishment. Don't forget the common sense part of our definition of behavior modification.

This definition of punishment can be diagrammed.

PUNISHMENT

Give:	Negative Reinforcer
	Or
Remove:	Positive Reinforcer

Becker provides a good summary regarding punishment.

Punishment is an effective method for changing behavior. However, because the person punished may learn to avoid and escape from the punisher, this is not usually a preferred method. There are problem behaviors where the use of punishment is the most humane thing that can be done. These problems usually involve very intense or very frequent problem behaviors. When punishment must be used, care must be taken to ensure its effectiveness and to minimize the development of avoidance behaviors.

Effective punishment:

1. is given immediately,
2. relies on withdrawal of reinforcers and provides clear steps for regaining them,
3. makes use of a warning signal,
4. is carried out in a calm, matter-of-fact way,
5. is accompanied by much reinforcement of behavior incompatible with the behavior being punished, and
6. also uses procedures to make sure that undesired behaviors do not receive reinforcement (1971).

In light of all this, why in the world do teachers continue to nag, yell, scream, etc.? In other words, why do they continue to use a negative reinforcer so often? Obviously *they* have been positively reinforced for it — after all, their behavior has increased in its use. Look at our diagram again from the teacher's viewpoint:

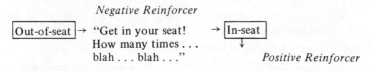

Negative Reinforcer

Out-of-seat → "Get in your seat! → In-seat
How many times . . .
blah . . . blah . . ." ↓

Positive Reinforcer

The teacher:
increases: yelling
decreases: ignoring out-of-seat
learns: yelling works!
feels: sad. "I wish
I didn't have
to yell so much."

Therefore, the next time the student is out-of-seat, she yells! Just like the proverbial vicious circle.

While we're at it, let's revamp the diagram as if the/teacher used positive reinforcers for good behavior and ignored undesirable behavior.

The student:
increases: in-seat
decreases: out-of-seat
learns: teacher attention is
             given only for in-seat.
feels: good because he re-
             ceived teacher praise.

Positive Reinforcer

Out-of-seat → "I see Mary is sitting down. Johnny is sitting, ready to begin reading. Look at Ed! How nice he looks at his desk . . ."

In-seat

Positive Reinforcer

The teacher:
increases: ignoring out-of-seat
           and praises in-seat
decreases: attention to
           out-of-seat
learns: behavior modifica-
           tion "works."
feels: pride in doing her
           job the right way to
           instill positive feel-
           ings in her students.

WHEN TO REINFORCE

While it is important to realize that positively reinforcing a response will tend to increase the recurrence of that response, it is just as important to know *when* to give the reinforcer. Certain *schedules* of reinforcement are appropriate depending on the behavior desired.

Skinner has discussed the value of knowing when to reinforce.

The nature or quantity of reinforcement is often much less important than the schedule on which it is received. Programming is again important, for many schedules can take effect only when the organism has passed through intervening contingencies. To take a very simple example – an apparatus which reinforces every hundredth response will have no effect at all if 100 responses are never emitted, but by reinforcing every second, then every fifth, then every tenth response, and so on, waiting until the behavior is well developed at each stage, we can bring the organism under control of the more demanding schedule (1963).

On a *continuous* reinforcement schedule, every response is reinforced. This schedule is used to obtain or to shape new behavior. Behavior learned under this approach extinguishes quickly as the behavior returns to the original level of occurrence rapidly.

On an *intermittent* reinforcement schedule only *some* responses are reinforced. This approach is used to maintain already learned behavior. Behavior learned under this schedule is quite resistant to extinction.

There are four types of intermittent reinforcement. Two of these have to do with the number of responses and are called ratio schedules; the other two have to do with the amount of time between reinforcers and are called interval schedules. Each type of reinforcement schedule, ratio and interval, can be fixed (reinforcement is presented at a predetermined or fixed time or with a predetermined or fixed number of responses) or it can be variable (reinforcement is presented on the basis of an average time or an average number of responses).

A *fixed ratio* schedule reinforces every nth response such as every tenth word spelled correctly. The more rapidly one works, the more he is reinforced. Any reduction in the tendency to respond results in no reinforcement. The less one responds, the less one gets.

A *variable ratio* schedule reinforces on the average of a certain number of responses, for example on an average of ten responses varying from six to twelve. Since the number of responses between reinforcements is variable, this generates a high rate of responding. Extinction is more difficult with a variable ratio schedule than with a fixed ratio schedule (Bijou and Baer, 1961). "Driven" behavior can be produced in the laboratory or in the classroom under this schedule. Such behavior might be considered similar to that of the compulsive gambler; he knows he will get his reward, but he must keep on keeping on until he gets it (Michael and Meyerson, 1966). This schedule of reinforcement might also explain the behavior of children who are labeled hyperactive or who have a short attention span.

A *fixed interval* schedule reinforces on the basis of the passage of time, such as every fifteen minutes. The amount of time is fixed or predetermined. A gold star presented to a child every hour for not chewing his pencil for that hour is an example of a fixed interval schedule. Behavior under this schedule is more resistive to extinction than behavior under a fixed ratio schedule.

Under this schedule, learning seems to slow down after each reward. People just do not seem to work as hard on Monday. Remember the spelling tests given every Friday? A high rate of studying occurs Thursday night just before the test the next day. Practically nobody studies spelling on Saturday night, or even on Monday night. Behavior is fairly inconsistent under this schedule but is also fairly predictable, dropping off immediately after the reward and gradually increasing up to the time that the reward is expected. The time that the reward is to be presented is known because the schedule is fixed.

A *variable interval* schedule of reinforcement is based on a variable amount of time having passed. The amount of time between reinforcers might vary from one minute to twenty minutes, only to have the next reinforcer occur after three minutes and the next after one hour. Usually the time between reinforcers is averaged to some predetermined amount of time. This schedule maintains a high degree of persistent behavior because the students never know for sure when the reward is going to occur. Take the case of the weekly spelling test on Friday. If the students did not know when the test was to be given, studying behavior would be maintained at a high level. One time it might be given after only one day, and the next time it might be given after three days have passed. In general, variable schedules generate great persistence in the face of non-reinforcement.

The following diagram summarizes the various types of intermittent reinforcement schedules:

INTERMITTENT REINFORCEMENT SCHEDULES

		Determinants	
		Passage of Time	Number of Responses
Frequency	Constant	Fixed Interval	Fixed Ratio
	Changeable	Variable Interval	Variable Ratio

IMPORTANCE OF THE STIMULUS

You have all seen the child who says, "Look at the doggie," when he sees a horse. This process is called *stimulus generalization.* It occurs when we respond to a similar stimulus in the same way we respond to the original stimulus. The student may call the letter "b" the letter "d," or he may be dependent on his mother at home and also is dependent on his teacher at school. All teachers are aware that such stimulus generalizations do occur. And because they do occur, many educators use this as a rationalization for not attacking school problems. "His home life is so bad that there is no wonder he acts as he does here at school. Therefore, I can't do anything about changing his behavior until his home life is improved."

Stimulus discrimination is another name for what you typically do in the classroom when you have to think up new ways to present the same topic over and over to the student who is having difficulty learning. There are many responses available to a given stimulus. The student "learns" the one which is reinforced. All of the possible responses seem to be competing for the reward. This competition slows down mastery. The student might ask himself, "Does 'but' spell /put/, /up/, /Tom/, /but/, /foot/, or what?"

The teacher's task is to prevent the competing responses from being expressed. Not reinforcing the incorrect response while reinforcing the correct response helps. In your method classes you probably learned various techniques to increase the "strength" of the stimulus. You might use colored chalk when printing the letter "b" in the word "but" in order to increase attention to the configuration of the letter or to increase the strength of the stimulus. You might use color only on the vertical stem of the letter. These techniques, and others, are used to prevent the competing response of the letter "p" from occurring. They bring the response under control of the stimulus.

The student learns that there is only one way to respond to each stimulus in order to be positively reinforced. The letter "b" is "b" and is not "p." In other words, certain behaviors are appropriate within a specific environmental context. Girls wear gloves to teas and not to play tennis. In instructional situations, reinforcement is given to the correct response, and all others are extinguished by not being reinforced. Stimulus discrimination is essentially a breakdown of generalization and is largely a matter of extinction (Keller, 1954; Clarizio and Yelon, 1967).

With the concept of stimulus discrimination in mind, we can now understand that the student who comes to school and shows dependence on the teacher because he is dependent on his mother at home must learn to discriminate one stimulus (mother) from the other (teacher). Because of this concept, the rationalization that the teacher cannot do anything with the student in school because of his home life becomes meaningless.

You all have experienced this learning. Remember when you were in junior high school and the first year you changed classes? It did not take you too long to learn that what you could get by with in one teacher's class you could not get by with in another. You learned through stimulus discrimination.

As mentioned previously, there are times when the desired response is not in the student's behavior repertory. In order to obtain the desired behavior, the existing behavior is reinforced *selectively* through the process called *successive approximation* until the desired behavior occurs. This process is referred to as *shaping*. Parents use successive approximation when their children begin talking.

"In teaching a child to talk, his efforts to pronounce a particular word will at first be reinforced rather uncritically. Eventually some of the variations will resemble accepted pronunciation more than others and receive selective reinforcement while other variations are allowed to extinguish. These events have the effect of producing a class of responses which come even closer to the correct pronunciation than the last reinforced response, and the selected reinforcement can be applied again" (Michael and Meyerson, 1966).

Johnston and others (1966) used this technique to get a nursery school boy to climb on the playground equipment. Reinforcement through smiling and talking to him was presented first when he was facing the direction of the equipment, then when he moved toward it, then when he placed his hand or foot on it, and finally when he was actually on it.

Chaffin and Kroth (1971) tell of using this approach in order to get a young girl to talk louder in class. She always whispered. The teacher began by leaning down very close so she could hear what the girl said. The next time, the teacher stood back about one foot and talked with the girl from that distance. The teacher gradually moved back during each conversation until the student was talking in a normal volume like the other students.

Another approach using successive approximation is to begin with the terminal behavior. For instance, if the desired behavior is putting on pants, begin with the pants in place, then lower them about two inches. When the child pulls them up and they are again in place, reinforce this small bit of behavior. Continue by lowering them by increasingly larger amounts, then off of only one foot, and finally off of the child entirely. The completion of each step reinforces that step and acts as a cue to progress to the next step until a reinforcement is received for the completion of the complex behavior. This process is called *chaining.* The more effective the reward, the more stable the chain of behaviors. Whenever behavior or a complex set of behaviors reliably occurs when the signal or cue is given, the behavior is said to be under *stimulus control.* In behavior modification, one of the goals is to get behavior under stimulus control.

CHAPTER IV

Modifying Behavior

IN A FEW MORE days your baseline period will probably be over and you will begin the actual behavior modification project. Remember that to show any change in the student's behavior you will have to continue to observe and record during the project just as you did during baseline.

As the time of the actual project draws near, you are probably becoming anxious to learn about practical applications and hints to make the project go smoothly in the classroom. You will learn about such things in this chapter.

TEACHERS AS BEHAVIOR MODIFIERS

By now you may be having some doubts about carrying out the project, or wondering if you should even try. Teachers are the very logical ones to incorporate the techniques of behavior modification into their instructional programs; in fact, you are ideal people to use behavior modification.

Altman and Linton (1971) gave three reasons why teachers and classrooms are ideally suited for using behavior modification. The school setting, especially the classroom, has traditionally been and presently is viewed as the place where children's social and academic behavior is modified. The classroom is a logical place because the students are mandated to attend school; consequently, in a sense you have a captive audience. There are certain state department curriculum requirements which you must meet through your instruction or through the modification of the student's behavior. The use of behavior modification techniques offers much promise for altering those behavior and academic problems that in the past resulted in exclusions from school or transfers to special classes. Other reasons have also been given for using behavior modification in school. "Some of the major advantages of its classroom use are the rapidity with which it has been used to modify many behaviors and the fact that its use does not tend to require such excessive individualized attention that the teacher must ignore other class members. Additionally, since in this model all behavior is viewed as normal, it does not seem to involve a basic alteration in the purposes of education for the teacher to attempt to modify those behaviors that interfere with the student's learning or the learning of his classmates" (Whitman and Whitman, 1971, p. 180).

The term behavior modification is used throughout this book, but sometimes the technique is referred to as contingency management. The relationship between the response and the reinforcement is called the *contingency*. When this contingency is controlled or managed, we have the process of behavior modification. The basic principle of operant conditioning demands that the consequences be contingent upon the occurrence of a specified behavior. Positive reinforcers, for example, are presented if, and only if, the behavior one is seeking to strengthen has occurred (Ross, 1967).

Another reason why teachers are logical people to use behavior modification is that the technique is easy to learn. Homme (1966) stated that while it takes years of graduate work to become an operant conditioner, teachers and parents can learn to become contingency managers within a period of hours or days since only the key bits of technology of operant conditioning are required. He feels that it is necessary for this learning to occur because teachers need to control behavior in the classroom. To become a contingency manager, all that is necessary is to take seriously the adage that "the likelihood that behavior will recur depends on its consequences." Reinforcing early in the game can make the difference between an effective and an ineffective contingency manager.

As you recall, behavior modification focuses on behavior rather than on its causes. Clarizio and Yelon (1967) gave several reasons why teachers are appropriate people to do this:

1. the teacher is not trained to probe the causes of behavior,
2. the teacher is rarely in a position to directly manipulate the causes such as a brain lesion or a faulty parent-child relationship,

3. maladaptive behavior may persist even if the cause could be manipulated (for instance, if the cause for poor reading were assumed to be poor vision and a faulty parent-child relationship, and the causes were corrected, the reading problem would still persist until attention had been directed to it),
4. current persisting symptoms may themselves be producing emotional disturbances,
5. there is no evidence to indicate that symptom substitution persists with behavior modification, and
6. the teacher has no resort other than to deal with behavior as it now appears since she cannot reshape the personality medically.

By now you should be convinced that behavior modification has something to offer and that you are an appropriate person to use it. You have labeled and defined the behavior and have observed and graphed it during the baseline period.

FINDING REINFORCERS

Now, what do you do? One of the first things to do is to find reinforcers. Finding the proper reinforcer to use can present a problem since what may be a positive reinforcer for one student may be a negative reinforcer for another. Taking a shower has been used as both a positive and a negative reinforcer. The trick is to know the student.

There are three things you can do to find reinforcers:

1. observe him; see what he chooses to do when he does not have to be doing something,
2. ask him what he would like to do,
3. ask his parents what some of his choice behaviors are.

In trying to find reinforcers, Homme (1966) suggests using the Premack Principle: for any pair of responses, the more probable one will reinforce the less probable one. He pointed out that if this is taken literally, the contingency manager will have thousands of reinforcers whereas he only had one or two before. Children often announce their own high probability behavior when they suggest some classroom activity they want to indulge in. Bricker reported several studies illustrating ways to find reinforcers.

Becker, Thomas, and Carnine (1969) gave an excellent summary of classroom procedures in using behavior modification. Their general rule for teachers is "Catch the children being good." They found that when and to whom the praise is given is more important than the amount. Their specific instructions to teachers were:

In general, give praise for achievement, prosocial behavior and following the group rules. Specifically, you can praise for concentrating on individual work, raising hand when appropriate, responding to questions, paying attention to directions and following through, sitting in the desk and studying, sitting quietly if noise has been a problem. Try to use variety and expression in your comments. Stay away from sarcasm. Attempt to become spontaneous in your praise, smile when delivering praise. At first you will probably get the feeling that you are praising a great deal and it sounds a little phony to your ears. This is a typical reaction and it becomes more natural with the passage of time. Spread your praise and attention around. If comments sometimes might interfere with the ongoing class activities, then use facial attention and smiles. Walk around the room during study time and pat or place your hand on the back of a child who is doing a good job. Praise quietly spoken to the children has been found effective in combination with some physical sign of approval.

They also gave the following instructions to teachers:

1. make explicit rules as to what is expected of children for each period. Remind them of the rules whenever this is needed.
2. *Ignore* (do not attend to) behaviors which interfere with learning or teaching unless a child is being hurt by another. Use punishment which seems appropriate, preferably withdrawal of some positive reinforcement.
3. give praise and attention to behavior which facilitates learning. Tell the child what he is being praised for. Try to reinforce behaviors incompatible to those behaviors you wish to decrease. Examples of how to praise:
   "I like the way you're working quietly."
   "That's the way I like to see you work."
   "Good job; you're doing fine."
   "I see Johnny is ready to work."
   "I'm calling on you because you raised your hand."
   "I wish everyone were working as nicely as Johnny."

There is a lot of talk nowadays about teacher expectancy. Students behave the way teachers expect them to behave. Brophy and Good (1970) studied this phenomenon in first grade classrooms and found that "teachers demanded better performance from those children for whom they had higher expectations and were more likely to praise such performance when it was elicited. In contrast, they were more likely to accept poor performance from those students when it occurred, even though it occurred less frequently." With knowledge of behavior modification, realizing that every student behaves in a certain way as a result of the consequences of that behavior, teacher expectancy can be drastically altered so that appropriate behavior, be it either social or academic, can be expected and properly reinforced for every student in the classroom.

INTERNAL AND EXTERNAL REINFORCEMENT

You might have asked yourself "What about the student who seems to learn on his own, seemingly without any reinforcer presented to him?" Some might argue that this student eventually does receive reinforcement from his peers for being a good student, from his teacher in the form of grades or recognition, from his parents, etc. Others would attribute this reinforcement as coming from within.

This study of control of behavior is referred to as "locus of control." "One of the personality constructs which seems likely to influence learning is 'internal-external locus of control' (I-E). It refers to the extent to which an individual feels that he has control over his behavior and its consequences. Internals (ILC) feel that the outcomes or reinforcements are the result of one's own behavior. Externals (ELC), on the other hand, believe that outcomes are independent of one's behavior and are the results of chance, fate, or powerful others" (Panda, 1971, p. 1). Studying educable mentally retarded children, Panda found that students considered to be either internals or externals did not differ on a game-type learning task. He did find that the offering of verbal support such as "You are doing well; good; very good," etc., tended to hamper rather than improve learning. These statements were *randomly* placed in the teacher's directions so that every student received some supportive statements.

Shaw and Uhl (1971) studied locus of control and socioeconomic levels. They found that second grade students with high external scores came mostly from the low socioeconomic level as compared with an upper-middle socioeconomic level. When just the upper-middle group was investigated, black students had higher external scores than white students. Race was not a factor in determining externals in the low socioeconomic level. Locus of control scores were not apparently related to IQ nor to sex.

While much more research will undoubtedly be done in this rather fascinating area, there are some implications for teachers who use behavior modification. It would appear that the high externals would be more receptive to tangible rewards for positive reinforcement. Also, they would be more likely to appreciate the praise given socially from the teacher for positive reinforcement. With this in mind, it might be that students from lower socioeconomic levels would be expected to respond positively to behavior modification techniques.

This, of course, does not mean that behavior modification should not be used with students from other socioeconomic levels. For some of these students, a reward system might be based on reinforcement which first comes as self-initiated and then from the teacher to support their own reward system without any feeling of being manipulated. This can easily be done by arranging a situation wherein the student is permitted to do something of his choice after having accomplished a certain task. Here, the reinforcement is not a physical object, but a privilege which he earned himself.

TOKEN REINFORCERS

Tangibles are typically used for reinforcers in the classroom. Usually they are such things as candy, toys, M & Ms, raisins, money, gold stars, stickers, etc. In the study of behavior modification, sometimes they, in addition to privileges, are earned only after a series of previous reinforcers have been received. Typically the previous reinforcers are tokens such as poker chips. The tokens are often accumulated to be turned in to the teacher to receive a more meaningful or "back-up" reinforcer. The back-up reinforcers can range from a single stick of gum to an expensive toy or to a pair of shoes or even to some special activity.

As inferred, tokens might be more appropriate for younger students from low socioeconomic levels. For other students, the social rewards typically found in a classroom just do not seem to serve as reinforcers of enough strength to perpetuate positive behavior. When tokens are used, they should be paired with the typical social reinforcers and then gradually withdrawn so that the social reinforcers become the conditioned reinforcers. Sattler and Swoope (1970) have given a procedural list of ten considerations for implementing a token reinforcement system:

1. select a method to choose the desirable behavior. This might be a value judgment and might involve the student.
2. select the type of token to use. They might be tally marks, poker chips, stars, etc.
3. select the back-up reinforcers for which the tokens can be exchanged.
4. select a cueing method for informing the students what behavior is to be reinforced. The goals should be made clear, possibly written on the board or in a book. The student should be told why he is being reinforced at the time the reinforcement is presented.
5. select a model for awarding tokens. This may be an admired student or the teacher.
6. construct a control sheet for recording the number of tokens given. The control sheet serves several purposes. With its use, tokens can be distributed to all members of the class for appropriate behavior. It serves as a monitor to the teacher by indicating how many tokens have been presented. It eliminates cheating, especially when the student has lost his control card.
7. schedule a time for the exchange of tokens. An appropriate time might

be the last twenty or thirty minutes of each school day. Leaders could be appointed to monitor the exchange.

8. select the method of making the back-up reinforcers available. The teacher might use a teacher's aide or a student teacher or leader in the classroom. There might be a "reinforcement area" in the back of the classroom for the sole purpose of the exchange.

9. devise a method of ending the reinforcement activity period. Even here, tokens might be given for putting things away properly in a positive manner.

10. select an appropriate contingency when awarding the tokens. This should be done for both individual and group reinforcement systems.

Tokens have typically been used on an individual basis. Studies regarding their use for the entire classroom are rare. A review of the literature by Altman and Linton resulted in "only two studies which have systematically investigated the effects of token reinforcers, as previously defined, on the classroom performance of the entire class in a public school setting" (Altman and Linton, 1971, p. 282).

Is It the Right Reinforcer?

As mentioned previously, it might be difficult to come up with reinforcers. Also, what might serve as a reinforcer one day might not serve as a reinforcer the next day or the next week. We all tire of the same type of reinforcers eventually. The teacher must be aware of when the strength of the chosen reinforcer is fading. This is the time to change the reinforcer. A cue to this change would be a drop in the frequency of the target behavior.

Holgate (1971) has prepared a table illustrating examples of both negative and positive reinforcers for a given event. (See page 50.)

In finding reinforcers, the teacher would be wise to try to see the world through the eyes of the target student. A teacher might think that an appropriate reward for Johnny would be to allow him to help grade papers. She established this contingency for some appropriate behavior only to find that Johnny's behavior did not improve. She, rather disgustedly, would probably conclude that there is not much to this behavior modification thing. On closer inspection, it might be revealed that grading papers was just what Johnny did not need to do since it earned him a great deal of harassment from the other boys in class whose approval was very important to him at that time. Many times when the teacher finds that the project that she has devised does not work, she has not actually chosen a positive reinforcer. Her values are different from the student's. That is

STIMULUS EVENTS AND EXAMPLES OF
POSITIVE AND NEGATIVE REINFORCERS
COMMONLY USED

Event	Positive Reinforcer	Negative Reinforcer
Talking out without permission	Answering *or* threatening without following through	Not answering *or* punishing as promised (e.g., removing privileges or having student leave group)
Correctly answering question	Saying immediately, "That is right."	Not commending student
Failing to have required supplies consistently	Allowing student to borrow supplies	Not allowing borrowing and/or giving failing daily grades
Disrespectful acts toward teacher	Entering into verbal argument with student *OR* giving lecture on bad manners	Ignoring student *OR* rapidly punishing student without verbal interchange
Inappropriate verbal behavior toward another student	Ignoring it or merely disapproving verbally	Immediate social isolation without verbal interchange
Turning in extra relevant work	Approval and public acknowledgement	Consistently failing to approve *OR* accusing student of "apple polishing"
Consistently not paying attention to directions and asking that they be repeated	Repeating directions *OR* mildly scolding child	Ignoring child and continuing with instructions

From S.H. Holgate, "Operant Principles and the Emotionally Disturbed Child," *Experimental Publication System,* April 1971, 11, Ms. No. 436-34. Copyright 1971 by the American Psychological Association and reproduced by permission.

why it is important to remember the three guides given earlier in finding reinforcers — namely: watch the student, ask the student, and ask his parents.

WHAT IF IT DOESN'T WORK?

Not only might the "reinforcement" actually chosen for a student turn out to be a flop, but the behavior of the teacher might be negatively reinforcing to the class as a whole. In these instances we usually find a teacher "who can't handle her class." This occurs even though the teacher has the best intentions, yet can't quite understand why her class is so disruptive.

When the teacher "simply can't figure it out," she would do well to look very carefully not only at the behavior of the students but at her own behavior as well. Then she should observe what happens before and after the events of concern to her.

Becker (1971) gives an excellent example of such a seemingly paradoxical situation.

The More Teachers Say "Sit-Down," the More They Stand Up

It was 9:20 a.m. in the first grade of forty-eight children taught by two teachers. Two rooms were available for the class with a movable wall between them. The children's desks were grouped into six tables of eight children each. They have been assigned work to do at their seats while the two young and capable teachers teach reading in small groups.

Two observers entered the room, sat down, and for the next twenty minutes they recorded the number of children out of their seats during each ten-second period. Observations were made for six days. The observers also recorded how often the teachers told the children to sit down, or to get back in their seats.

During the first six days about three children were out of their seats every ten seconds. The teachers would say "sit down" about seven times in a twenty-minute period.

Then some very strange events began to occur. The teachers were asked to tell the children to "sit down" more often. During the next twelve days the teachers said "sit down" 27.5 times each twenty minutes. The children stood up more – an average of 4.5 children standing every ten seconds.

Again, we asked the teachers to tell the children to "sit down" more often (twenty-eight times in twenty minutes). *The children stood up more again* – four times every ten seconds.

Finally, we asked the teachers to quit telling the children to sit down, but rather to praise sitting and working. They did this well, and less than two children were standing every ten seconds, the lowest standing observed . . .

The teacher's saying "sit down" *follows* standing up. When the teacher says "sit down" more often, the children stand up more often. When the teacher says "sit down" less often, the children stand up less often. "Sit down" is a reinforcing consequence for standing up. "Sit down" is an event following a response which strengthens that response. It *is* a reinforcer for standing up.

But "sit down" also has another effect on the response of sitting. The children do sit down when told to, so "sit down" must *also* be a signal for sitting.

What a beautiful trap! Imagine, the teacher thinks that telling the children to "sit down" works, because they *do sit down*. But that is only the immediate effect. The effect on standing is not seen until later and might be missed unless you learn what to look for. The teacher's words are having exactly the opposite effect on standing from that which she desires (Becker, 1971, pp. 85-86).

You will recall that in the previous chapter a similar situation was presented in the discussion on negative reinforcers. Here, the teacher also learned that yelling "sit down" works, and she will continue to do so over and over and over again.

MODELING

The finding of a positive reinforcer may take the form suggested by Clarizio and Yelon (1967) called *modeling*. This is one of the two contributions to the field of behavior modification which has come from work solely with human subjects. The other is social reinforcement (Wolf and Risley, 1967).

Clarizio and Yelon (1967) cite three effects as a result of exposure to models:

1. *modeling effect.* Children acquire responses that were not part of their behavior. When this method is combined with verbalization, it quickly produces new behavior.
2. *inhibitory or disinhibitory effect.* This is known as the strengthening or inhibiting of responses already existing in the observer of the model. When children see the model rewarded, they copy the behavior; when the model is punished, they eliminate that behavior.
3. *eliciting effect.* The teacher elicits the response that closely or precisely matches that of the model from the observing child. This behavior is not new to the observer, and it has not been previously punished.

In a review of the literature on behavior modification, Altman and Linton (1971) discuss modeling as "vicarious reinforcement." Their studies pointed out that the effects of modeling are not long lasting and that it must be followed by positive reinforcement to the student who is observing the model.

Comments like "I like the way Mary is studying" serve to indicate to other students that Mary in this case is a model for "studying" behavior. Again, the teacher must be careful not to point out an inappropriate model. Even though her behavior is appropriate, Mary would not be a good model if she were not liked by the other students in the room. You can imagine the effect of "Now be a good boy like Bobby" if Bobby was the kid you were waiting to beat up after school.

Adults serve as models for students, also. Typically adult models are most apparent in the adolescent years during the "hero worship" stage. The young athlete mocks the stance and idiosyncrasies of the coach; the young girl begins to wear her hair like the home economics teacher.

Oftentimes we overlook the most simple or the most logical approach to the modification of behavior – the stimulus. Stimulus material such as teacher-made ditto sheets, crafts materials, the work books, teacher lectures and directions, etc., when altered, may in fact, modify student behavior. Teacher instructions, a common stimulus, may be too complex for students to sort out the various meanings and steps involved to complete the tasks required. You all know the student whose behavior is negative because the work is too easy – he's bored. Usually more challenging material of his interest will spark a degree of motivation.

But what about the student who is having difficulty in achievement? He appears to be disinterested and sometimes is aggressive. Kroth (Chaffin and Kroth, 1971) tells the story about the. teacher of an educable mentally retarded class who was upset at the lack of success that one boy was having. She felt that he did not pay attention and had a short attention span. The particular task of concern was tying yarn to a coat hanger to make a duster. Upon observation, it was found that the yarn was cut into pieces only two inches long. The boy had difficulty manipulating yarn of this short size. When four inch yarn was substituted, the teacher noted that he became less distractable and enjoyed the project.

In a two-year study of emotionally disturbed children in self-contained special classes in a public school system, Glavin, Quay, and Werry (1971) used behavior modification techniques to control deviant behaviors. During the second year which emphasized academic achievement, the writers noticed a significant improvement in behavior. They interpreted their findings as refuting the belief that deviant behavior needs to be changed prior to stressing academic achievement. During the second year, fewer instances of "blow-up" behavior occurred.

Properly presented academic instruction at the student's level of mastery, when paired with an instructional strategy of behavior modification technique, seems to be quite effective not only in increasing academic achievement but also in increasing preferred behavior. With careful attention to the stimulus material, this alone sometimes does wonders.

ANOTHER WAY TO CHANGE BEHAVIOR: DIAGNOSTIC/PRESCRIPTIVE TEACHING

Concerned teachers ask themselves "WHY isn't Johnny learning?" Typical answers given to them might say because he is emotionally disturbed, is mentally retarded, has a learning disability, or some such response. Such labeling does not give the teacher any direction for instruction. The problem might be that the wrong question was asked. To paraphrase Kennedy: "Ask not: WHY isn't Johnny learning, ask: HOW does Johnny learn?" Only after this question is answered can an appropriate instruction take place. Diagnostic/prescriptive teaching provides a framework within which a teacher can determine how the student learns and subsequently choose appropriate instructional strategies to use with the student.

Diagnostic/prescriptive teaching is an ongoing process wherein instructional strategies are matched to the student's unique learning mode.

The initial task for the diagnostic/prescriptive (D/P) teacher is to determine the unique learning mode of the student. A learning mode is that pattern of relationships among Input, Process, and Output which serve to effect desired behavioral change. Input has to do with sensory information received from visual, auditory, or haptic stimuli; Process concerns the manipulation of the sensory data; Output concerns the responses resulting from Input and Process. A typical model to reflect these procedures might look like this:

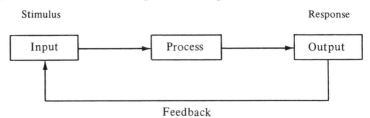

Stimulus   Response

Feedback

The defining of a student's learning mode is accomplished by determining how the student receives, processes, and expresses information. We do this by using various diagnostic activities. Most of the activities will be of an informal nature devised by the D/P teacher since there are no standardized tests available for teacher use which are specified for such a purpose. General achievement test batteries give results in broad areas of achievement. The "diagnostic" batteries specify achievement in more refined skill areas. With results from standardized and individually administered diagnostic tests, the D/P teacher knows achievement strengths and weaknesses of the student.

If the results of a diagnostic reading test suggest that the student cannot read words containing certain blends, a teacher would proceed to teach those blends. It is quite possible that the teacher might soon ask the question "WHY isn't Johnny learning the blends?" It could be that the teacher is teaching them the wrong way. In other words, since she has no information to define the learning mode of the student, she could be using an inappropriate instructional strategy. She had not matched her instructional strategy to the unique learning mode of the student because she did not know what his learning mode was. Data from general achievement batteries and from diagnostic tests alone do not give enough information for a teacher to determine a student's learning mode nor to select an appropriate instructional strategy to use. Unfortunately, this is as far as many remedial programs have gone. It might account for their lack of success.

The D/P teacher must integrate information received from many different sources with the information she- receives from her informal diagnostic activities to answer the question of *how* Johnny learns. To better determine what diagnostic activities to use, an understanding of the pattern of a learning mode is in order.

The learner receives information visually, auditorily, or haptically. (For our purposes, we are not considering smelling or tasting which might be appropriate stimuli in certain situations.) He then associates the new information with previously learned information and responds verbally or motorically.

The learning mode, then, reflects the nature of the tasks on which the student is most successful. If the task consists primarily of auditory input (stimulus) with verbal output (response) such as when the teacher asks a question and the student responds verbally, the task is called auditory-verbal. The first term, "auditory," defines the input channel, and the second term, "verbal," defines the output channel. The game of "Simon Says" is an auditory-motor task when the teacher gives verbal direction for the student to place both hands on his head.

As you can well imagine, there are many input and output combinations tasks. Also, different processing might be required for each unique combination. It stands to reason that the input channels of vision and hearing as well as the output channels of talking and movement must be such that the material actually presented is correctly received and that the intended response is correctly made. If these channels of reception and expression are functioning adequately, we then might be able to infer the methodology of processing which the student uses.

To receive the stimulus material the eye must be a healthy organ. Visual acuity must be within normal range either naturally or with corrective lenses. These points are rather easily determined by evaluation by specialists. Even with a healthy eye and with good visual acuity, a "vision problem" might still exist when one considers the functional use of the eyes. Students who use their eyes inappropriately, for whatever reason, will have difficulty in receiving the stimulus material which is presented visually. The American Optometric Association* has studied this aspect of education quite extensively and has literature available on the subject for teachers.

A word of caution is in order, however. Some teachers and parents can quickly explain away the "reason" for a reading problem by attributing it to a vision problem. They may be only half correct. The visual stimulus material must be correctly received by the student before learning to read can occur. The reading process requires more than proper visual reception, but improper visual reception can impede the reading process. Consequently, when the visual stimulus material is matched to the student's unique visual characteristics, reading behavior is more likely to be improved.

*American Optometric Association, 7000 Chippewa St., St. Louis, Mo. 63119.

A similar line of thinking applies to auditorily presented stimulus material. To properly receive auditory information, the hearing mechanism must be healthy with good auditory acuity either naturally or with a corrective hearing aid. Functional use of hearing implies good auditory discrimination and adequate "emotional adjustment" (appropriate behavior). Language, culture, socioeconomic level, all enter into the field of study and relate to the use of auditory material, becoming quite complex. The Illinois Test of Psycholinguistic Abilities (Kirk, McCarthy, and Kirk, 1968), offers an excellent model relative to the use of auditory and visual skills. Materials have been developed which align closely to these various psycholinguistic processes (Karnes, 1968). As with vision, the auditory stimulus material must be matched to the unique hearing and language characteristics of the student. The American Speech and Hearing Association* can be of service to teachers in this area.

Likewise, speech represents the verbal mode of expression. Articulation problems interfere with fluent expression. Many parents and teachers become unduly concerned over simple articulation errors which are easily overcome by age or by speech therapy. Delayed speech, immature speech patterns, and general language are more complex components of verbal expression.

Consideration of cultural and socioeconomic level should be given before any possible erroneous interpretation is made about the potential for academic learning or about academic learning that has been achieved.

In much the same way, movement is the nonverbal expression of learning. Handwriting and gestures are commonly observed in the classroom as indications of learning. The range from gross physical impairment to minor clumsiness can account for problems with motor expression. The medical history of the learner as well as his general maturity level would be important information to have prior to judging the adequacy of his motor expression. Akin to motor expression, knowledge of perceptual-motor development is vital in diagnostic teaching. Kephart (1971) outlined this developmental aspect of education and has related it to the instructional process. Roach and Kephart (1966) devised an observational scale for teachers to use to help observe various facets of perceptual-motor behavior.

In order to develop a frame of reference for D/P teaching, we need to give some consideration to diagnostic activities. Diagnostic activities can be considered as those careful and critical procedures of observation, the purpose of which is to determine if a *pattern* of behavior exists. There usually is a pattern to the behavior of students. Such a pattern usually is found within all three domains, cognitive, affective, and psycho-motor. The pattern is rather stable and usually makes sense to the student. Our task is to find out just what that "sense" is. We do this by diagnostic Looking, Asking, and Listening.

*American Speech and Hearing Association, 9030 Old Georgetown Road, Washington, D.C. 20014.

LOOKING. Looking (observation) was discussed earlier in this book. We learned that students tell us many things by what they do. This is true in academic related behavior as well as when the student is on the playground or talking with his friends. The student gives us cues to his unique learning characteristics. To pick up these cues we need to sharpen up our observation skills. Cues to the student's unique learning characteristics can be obtained by critically observing the *product* of his learning. Try to determine if an error pattern exists.

Do reading errors occur more frequently on the final sounds of words? Is the division answer incorrect because of errors in multiplication? If so, on what facts does he err? Is there an isolated letter which is exceptionally troublesome in penmanship?

We also obtain cues to the student's characteristics by observing him *while* he is performing the academic task. Does he count on his fingers? Does he move his lips when he reads silently? Does he hold the book at an unusual angle? Does he stumble on a certain pattern of words when he reads orally? The teacher who sends the student back to his desk to work alone while he grades papers is missing out on a lot of diagnostic information. Let the student work at least a few of the problems at your desk, or in any situation where you can spend a few minutes observing him *while* he is working.

We obtain additional cues (maybe the most important cues) by observing, that is *looking at* the student, during the instructional presentation which is *while* you are actually teaching. The teacher might also look at the student's behavior in terms of his preferred *situational* mode of learning. Does he perform better in a one-to-one setting? If so, whom does he work well with? Teacher? Peer? Teacher aide? Volunteer? Parent? etc. Does he prefer a small group, large group, or to work independently? Finally, some observations should be made to determine what type of reinforcers are serving to maintain the particular behavior that is of concern to the teacher. These reinforcers can be available from other students in the classroom, from the teacher, or from some other part of the environment. Diagnostic Looking might help you find some of the answers. Error patterns that we observe in our diagnostic looking usually make some sort of sense to the student. Since it is your task to determine just what that "sense" is, one of the easiest ways to find out is to ask him.

ASKING. The second way of determining an established pattern of behavior is through the process of diagnostic questioning or of asking. Often this is the most direct route, and many times the easiest way, to determine what a student's error pattern might be. Instead of following the typical procedure of telling the student what to do, checking his work, putting a grade on the paper, and handing it back to him, the D/P teacher uses questioning to get the student to explain his processing. The teacher might ask questions such as these: "Would you explain to me what you have just finished doing? Have you ever seen this problem before? Tell me what goes here. Show me how you regroup these items. How did you get your answer. Tell me what is wrong with this problem. What do you not understand in this problem? Why did you ____? Where did you get the ____? Tell me what you should do next. Draw me a picture of this problem."

The wording of a question tends to elicit a particular type of response. Even though the anticipated response will be either verbal or motor, you might expect one and get the other. The response gives you a clue to the student's preferred mode of learning. Teacher directions, like questions, also elicit certain expected responses. The learning mode for some students appears to be mostly visual: they learn more easily from what they see rather than from what they hear. Others learn mostly from listening. The response mode can vary with either of these two types of learners.

All types of diagnostic questions tend to increase student involvement in the learning process. When students are involved, they tend to be more motivated for doing the work. When they are motivated, they tend to see the relevance of the tasks. When tasks are relevant, less disruption is displayed and greater achievement is observed.

LISTENING. The third type of diagnostic activity is listening. Many times teachers "listen" with their "third ear." They are auditorily "reading between the lines." Maybe we can say they are "listening between the words." Does Johnny's question mask his real concern or his real question? When he asks "What time is Gym?" he might be wanting to know how much longer he has to spend at an undesirable task. The query of "Do teachers think stealing is a sin?" might be meant to inquire if the teacher would like him if the teacher knew that he had stolen something over the weekend.

We must determine if a student's question might be for the sole purpose of obtaining immediate information so he can get down to bigger and better things. There are times when a teacher has expounded on a topic and has gone into long detail on some issue in order to "teach" something when the student only wanted a simple yes or no answer.

You might need to determine if Susie wants to tell you something in secret just because she wants to share something with you and with nobody else, or if she is afraid of what her peers might think about what she had to say.

Listen to the response given by the student before you judge it as inappropriate or incorrect. It might be that you asked the question in the wrong way for that particular student. Could he be creative and thinking of some relationship which does not make sense to you, but does make sense to him? How do you respond to the "silly" answer? Sometimes a simple comment such as "Could you explain that to the class" might serve to clarify a possible misunderstanding on either the student's part or perhaps on the teacher's part. It might also clarify if the student is being a smart-alec at that moment.

We have been talking about certain aspects of the "diagnostic" part of the total diagnostic/prescriptive teaching process. Diagnosis is conducted for the sole purpose of prescription development to be used in remediation or in circumvention of the problem. Having established the learning mode as a result of diagnostic activities, the teacher then draws upon a rich background of training and experience to determine which instructional strategies to match to the student's learning mode. When such a match occurs, learning is more likely to be ensured. The instructional strategies are, in a sense, PRESCRIBED by the results of the diagnostic activities, especially the learning mode.

STIMULUS MATERIAL

The prescriptive aspect of the diagnostic/prescriptive process must take into account the stimulus materials used in your instruction. The materials lend themselves to particular types of instructional directions, questions, and consequently responses. Some materials can be used in a variety of ways. A knowledge of a variety of materials and how they might be used makes the instructional process easier.

The point to remember is that the stimulus material must match the unique learning mode of each student. Often this means going beyond the usual procedure of placing a student in the front row so that he can hear better or of providing him with a large print textbook so that he can see better.

Once you feel fairly confident that you know the unique learning mode of the student, have selected appropriate stimulus material and have matched an instructional strategy to his unique characteristics, you have an approach which is more likely to ensure learning. The creating of this total approach is sometimes called educational prescription development. The educational prescription goes further than simply matching stimulus material to the learner.

With the match of material and learner you can now *begin* your instructional sequence which will probably be aimed at remedying certain academic weaknesses. As you proceed you will want to consider building new ways of learning for the student so that he will be able to learn from an instructional presentation that would be given to the more typical student.

Beginning remediation uses the student's unique learning characteristics to strengthen or expand other learning modes which the student does not presently display. In this way, remediation can take place while concurrently he is learning other ways to learn. This strategy is for the purpose of developing new learning modes so that typical classroom group instruction will be effective for the student.

It is beyond the scope of this book to go into the intricacies of the study of learning disabilities. It would seem that all teachers would profit from a graduate level course in learning disabilities to better enable them to determine what stimulus material would be appropriate for each student. After all, the teacher's task is to modify behavior, including academic behavior, and the use of appropriate material can help you do this.

When teaching, don't forget to call on other school and community specialists to be of assistance to you. The school psychologist, the speech therapist, the school nurse, and the school social worker are vital resource personnel who can be of assistance in these matters.

Another aspect of diagnostic/prescriptive teaching so often overlooked is that of the developmental level of the student.

Many teachers seem to choose activities at a level beyond the developmental age of many students. This is probably because of the traditional viewpoint of matching certain predetermined achievement levels with certain chronological ages without considering the developmental aspects of growth. The Gesell Institute for Child Development* has information for teachers which might guide them in selecting appropriate instructional strategies and in selecting appropriate stimulus material. Ilg and Ames (1965) have described certain scholastic-related activities by various age levels. Ames (1968) has discussed the relationship of developmental characteristics to learning disabilities.

An instructional presentation requires mastery of previously presented stimulus material. When prior mastery has not occurred, the current stimulus material becomes confusing and meaningless to the student. If this is the case, then consider dropping back to the previous level of material which is a prerequisite. You can continue in this way until you find a level of achievement that the student has mastered. From this point you can build your instructional strategy in a hierarchically arranged sequence of steps moving to the next level of difficulty only after mastery of the prior level. Gagne (1965) has outlined a sequence of conditions of learning which the teacher presents in an orderly fashion to more successfully ensure mastery.

If we believe that the changing of behavior is the sine qua non of teaching, it should be remembered that behavior modification does not stand alone, in isolation from a knowledge of educational psychology, child development, teaching methodology, and common sense.

SOME EXAMPLES

Teachers are always interested in what other teachers have done in their classrooms, especially if what they have done actually produces a positive change in their students. It would be appropriate now to review briefly some work that has been done by other researchers to illustrate the varied approaches to behavior modification that have been used successfully. The range and the techniques are limited only by the creativity of the teacher.

*Gesell Institute for Child Development, 310 Prospect St., New Haven, Conn. 06511.

Almost any "problem" behavior has been dealt with through behavior modification. Bijou (1965) worked with parent-child relationships in a clinical setting, the guidance of preschool children in a nursery school setting, the treatment and rehabilitation of severely disturbed young children in a residential institution, the training of retarded children in reading, writing, and arithmetic in a school for the retarded, and the analysis of conceptualization behavior in normal and retarded children in a laboratory situation.

Zimmerman and Zimmerman (1966) found that smiles, chatting, and teacher proximity served as reinforcers in dealing with spelling errors, temper tantrums, irrelevant verbal behavior, and baby talk in special education classrooms for emotionally disturbed preadolescents.

In a classroom of students with average ability who were educationally retarded and described as minimally brain damaged, McKenzie and others (1967) used grades to obtain a specified monetary allowance from parents. The children were given weekly assignments in the five areas of reading, arithmetic, spelling, penmanship, and English composition. Each subject area had one sheet listing the materials to be used and the total number of responses that were assigned. The children recorded their starting and finishing times. All of the work on each sheet had to be completed before going on to new work. The students were scored as "attending" if they were sitting at their desks with materials open and before them and eyes directed toward the materials. Contact with the teacher or the teacher aides also was scored as proper attending, as was orientation toward the work materials or to a reciting fellow student or teacher if they were responding orally to a lesson in a group situation.

This project is a good example of how the describing of "attention" can actually be written so that it can be observed. It is also interesting to note that the use of academic work alone increased attention to the task. The students earned the privilege of recess if all of the assignments were completed; if the assignments were not completed, they worked through recess. Free time was granted if the work was finished before study time was over. If the work was completed before lunch, the students got to eat in the school cafeteria; if not, they ate alone at their desk. Throughout the project, teacher attention was given to the appropriate behavior only.

For those of you who shudder at the thought of paying students for grades, you might be surprised to learn that this approach was found to be useful in this situation. Grades were sent home weekly. The parents paid the students according to the grades they received for the week. This was a substitute for allowances. If some work was incomplete, the parents subtracted accordingly from the amount of money given to the child. No other money could be earned at home. Any presents of money were banked. This approach kept money as a high level reinforcer, thereby serving to increase academic behavior at school. The researchers found that attending behavior increased for both reading and arithmetic.

In another study by Wolf and Risley (1967) points were given for those students in their seat when the signal of a buzzer was given. The buzzer was activated on the average of twenty-minute intervals to control out-of-seat behavior. In one case, the four children sitting around a difficult student were rewarded along with her. The praise and nagging from the peers were effective in maintaining her in-seat behavior.

In a similar study, Wolf and others (1970) gave points to students who were in their seats every time a buzzer sounded. It was arranged that the buzzer would go off on the average of every twenty minutes. The actual sounding of the buzzer ranged from zero to forty minutes. However, there was one student for whom this approach was not too successful. The student was given fifty points to start with. Each time she was out of her seat, she would lose ten points. The buzzer, for her, was sounded on the average of every ten minutes. To make this method even more effective, the four students around her were involved. The total number of points she earned would be divided by the four students surrounding her. It seems that the peer influence did have an effect in controlling her behavior. If she stood up, the students reminded her to sit down. Some even offered to sharpen her pencil for her in order for her to remain in her seat. The classroom teacher probably appreciated this amount of peer influence.

Tokens were used as reinforcers in a study by Tyler and Brown (1968) with court-committed boys ages thirteen to fifteen years in a training school. Comparing the group receiving tokens as reinforcers for high test scores with the group receiving tokens merely as "straight salary," the conclusion was that the contingent token reinforcement strengthened academic performance.

Morice (1968) cites evidence of the value of behavior modification with first graders to control attention, disruptive behavior, temper tantrums, and talking; with a fourth grader to gain cooperation; and with a bright sixth grader to increase work output. Inaccuracies on weekly spelling tests were reduced by using pony rides only if the student scored at least 75 per cent correct. For the twenty-four weeks following the program, the student fell below this level only three times. This is one of the many studies which incorporate parent cooperation to help in the reinforcement system in order to modify behavior while at school.

Becker, Thomas, and Carnine (1969) give several interesting examples of the use of behavior modification. One student was aggressive in the classroom and did not complete his class assignments. On days that he worked diligently and was cooperative, the teacher sent a note home. With this note he was permitted to watch TV for a designated amount of time.

With a fourth grader from a deprived background who dawdled instead of working and who displayed aggressive behavior toward younger children, check marks were placed on the board when he displayed ten minutes of good working behavior. If he earned ten checks, he could spend thirty minutes in the kindergarten room supervising younger boys in the use of carpentry tools. His behavior improved, and he became quite a star to the younger boys. A similar approach might be used, with the reward being the privilege to participate in a cross-age tutoring session or "teaching" younger students.

Patrol boys, instead of acting as policemen, reported the names of children who left and returned to school displaying good behavior instead of fighting. The class with the most names reported won a banner for a week. ·

One boy, who liked to fight, earned an "X" on the board for every half day in which he did not fight. When he accumulated four Xs, he earned a party for the entire class, and he got to play host by passing out cookies.

Fox (1966) applied the technique of successive approximation to increase study skills with the SQ3R reading method. This method has the student survey the material to be read, ask questions to himself about the material, read, recite to himself what he read, and finally review what he read.

In a graduate class taught by this writer which had studied behavior modification, one teacher reported that she was concerned with the noise level of her classroom. She decided to give "free talk time" at the end of the class period if the class refrained from undue talking until that time. This was a class of junior high English students who were more interested in the social activities of the school than in the subject of English. The teacher considered that she spent fifteen minutes of class time telling the class to be quiet. She gave the class five minutes of visitation time following what she considered a good attentive period. The teacher gained ten minutes of class time, and the students were more productive during class and appreciated and looked forward to the five minutes of free time thereafter.

Another teacher decided to buy the students who obtained 98 per cent correct on the Friday spelling test an ice cream cone during the lunch period at school. This grade four class responded favorably, and the expense account of the teacher rose, as did the grades for the students in her room.

A program that has been used to teach in-seat behavior or any other approved behavior is to set a kitchen timer according to a variable schedule specified by the program. When the bell rings, the teacher looks up at the child and determines whether reinforcement is due or not. If the child is showing the proper behavior when the bell goes off, the teacher nods to the child to cue him to record a mark on the chart on his desk. When the chart is filled, the child can spend the points earned for a preselected activity or for tangibles. The program slowly increases the time between bells, then step by step fades out the timer, the chart, the points, and eventually the special reinforcers. Social reinforcement must be paired with the tangible reinforcers in order for the social reinforcers alone to become meaningful.

Using marks on the board for every five or ten minutes of good working behavior can be a way for the class to earn extra minutes at recess or play time. A teacher might also use the same approach in order to decrease the amount of recess time; but which is the more positive? It goes without saying that the administration must be willing for the teacher to experiment with some of these methods.

Remember that we stated that the teacher should try to look at reinforcers from the viewpoint of the student? Sometimes what we think are reinforcers actually are not, and then we make statements that the behavior modification thing does not work. In a case study presented by Holmes (1966) with a nine year old underachiever who displayed behavior problems, such a situation actually occurred.

The student intentionally disturbed the classroom and displayed antosocial behaviors which were rewarded by social recognition and attention from his peers. It seems that the "punishment" used by school personnel was quite rewarding to him. When the teacher purposefully withdrew attention from these behaviors, they became worse. The attention he had gained earlier was not given, so he became more disruptive to ensure that he would at least gain some sort of attention; he just had to work harder to get it. A logical solution was to keep him in after school (we all have tried that). However, this did not work because he obtained the attention from his mother who would drive to school to pick him up. Arrangements were later made for him to ride home on the bus with students he did not know.

But the behavior in the classroom was shifted to foolish errors on only one or two spelling words which the teacher knew that he could spell correctly. In the teacher's mind the errors "did not make any sense." As you all know by now all behavior makes sense to the student, it is up to us to make sense out of the behavior. But why should a student purposefully make errors on a spelling test?

It so happened that the teacher had determined that whoever got 100 per cent of the spelling words correct got to serve as class monitor. The responsibility of the class monitor was to report any misbehavior to the teacher. This student valued the friendship of his peers and did not want to be placed in the position to "squeal" on his friends! The teacher changed the contingency to allow him to erase the chalkboard if he achieved 100 per cent correct on his spelling test thereafter. He quite nicely complied with this arrangement.

One boy was sent to the social worker every time he had a temper tantrum. The tantrums seemed to increase. It was decided that the boy would have to earn time with the social worker by showing progressively improved classroom behavior. The tantrums soon subsided. This might also work for the youngster who is frequently sent to the principal's office for maladaptive behavior.

Can you imagine a situation in which you would *not* recommend to parents that they help the poor reader at home? Curry (1970) made such a recommendation in his case study of an eight year old student who was repeating the second grade. The baseline study investigated the student's rate and the number of errors made. Even with a low rate and a high number of errors, she often volunteered to read aloud in class and to her parents at home. It was thought that this poor reading behavior was a method for her to gain the attention of the listeners. Therefore, it was recommended that she do no reading at home, receive no extra instructions, that all errors were ignored, and that she could read only until she made five errors at which time she had to stop. Within three weeks the rate increased from 20 to 100 words per minute with a drop in errors from 25 per cent to less than 5 per cent. At the end of the school year a gain of two years had been made in six months time.

Allen, Turner, and Everett (1970) reported using behavior modification techniques in a Head Start Program with a particularly disturbing student called Townsend. Their study is a good example of the application of shaping, successive approximation, fading, and extinction in a very practical situation. Townsend liked to throw temper tantrums, and occasionally they were quite severe and naturally disruptive. On these occasions the teacher took the rest of the class out to play leaving Townsend inside the room. When the tantrum indicated a lessening up, he was asked if he would like to go out and play. If the tantrum began anew, she would turn away in order not to give attention to the unwanted behavior and wait until he quieted down before she asked again. From a tantrum lasting twenty-seven minutes, with this technique the third day found one mild tantrum of four-minutes' duration, with none thereafter.

Townsend also liked to assault other children. The teacher would purposefully turn her back to Townsend and give her attention to the other child attacked. After two weeks, a decline in this behavior was noted, and no other assault occurred.

Townsend rode the bus to school. You might imagine the behavior he displayed. He would get out of his seat belt, try to open the door, try to play with the instrument panel, throw himself at the driver, and display other generally disruptive acts. Ten days after a rather individualized program had begun, Towsend was no longer the problem he initially was on the bus. How can behavior change over such a short period of time? What did the teacher do?

On the first day, the teacher buckled him in his seat belt, put a peanut in his mouth to serve as an immediate tangible reinforcer, and said something like, "Good! You are sitting quietly, all buckled up snug in your seat belt." She was wise to quickly give a peanut to the other students on the bus praising them for being quiet. She did this on approximately twenty to ninety second intervals throughout the fifteen minute bus ride.

This type of reinforcement continued on the second day through the fifth day, gradually increasing the amount of time between peanuts. On the sixth through the eighth day, the peanuts were given when the students got off of the bus. On the ninth day, there were no peanuts. But the driver praised the students, who were met at the bus stop by the teacher who gave them a lollipop. The good behavior on the bus continued without the intensive program which had begun only nine days earlier.

This study also reports the shaping of socialization by teaching how to play, first alone, then with one other child, and then gradually with others. Motor skills and appropriate verbal behavior and comments also were gradually developed and shaped using basic behavior modification techniques. The examples reported above cover a range of applications from the very simple to quite complex programs of behavior modification. Behavior modification is a technique that is useful for those unique cases that require a carefully planned program of implementation. It must be more than that though. It should become a natural part of your minute-to-minute instructional methodology. Hopefully, if it does, you will not need to develop a more complex program.

HOW CAN I USE IT?

We have looked at situations where carefully planned programs had been developed. But how can one use the techniques in a routine, matter of fact way in those thousand of interactions that occur daily in a classroom?

Remember that one basic underlying factor is a change of viewpoint on the teacher's part. Look for the positive rather than the negative. Think about the number of correct responses rather than the number of errors that a student makes and mark papers accordingly. Attend to the positive behavior rather than the negative. This is not easy to do, and no one pretends that it *is* easy. Teaching is no gravy train; yet it can be a rewarding (reinforcing) experience if we allow it to be.

You all probably have or will develop your own techniques to get the class organized in preparation for some activity such as reading time, reading circles, math worksheets, recess, lunch room time, clean-up time, art, etc., etc. Why not use the organization time in a behavior modification sense?

"Row one can line up first because the desks are cleaned off."

"Mary's reading group may come first because everyone has his book out."

"Susie may pass out the math pages because she has worked hard this morning." (How many times have you given the math pages to Johnny to pass out because he was causing a disturbance in the back of the room and you wanted to stop it?)

"Johnny's group may use the kiln today because everyone read well this morning."

"The row that gets the paste washed off the desks first gets to go to lunch first."

"Bill gets a free night with no algebra homework because all of his daily work has been correct for the week."

"Dorothy, Eddie, and Tom may listen to records for the next fifteen minutes because they did a good job in cleaning up the room."

etc.
etc.
etc.

What about the student who is always raising his hand for me to come to his desk to check out every arithmetic problem he does? Why does he do this?

Attention probably. Especially if most of the problems are correctly done. Chaffin and Kroth (1971) offered an approach for the teacher to use in this situation. You might say something like, "Now work this next one by yourself while I check on Susie's paper." Go back to him afterwards and mark the problem; then say, "I've got to check on some other papers. You do the next two and I'll be right back." Gradually fade out your attention, and then you can correct up to five, then up to ten problems, and eventually the entire paper without having to return to his desk to check out every one.

You might know a student who does not sustain his attention throughout long assignments. While his attention to the task can be lengthened by the use of behavior modification techniques, you will have to begin facing the fact that he is displaying a short attention span and start from there. In our discussion of the effect of the stimulus material on behavior, you recall that a change in the material might also effect a change in behavior. Some students, when presented with an entire page of problems or an assignment too lengthy, can correctly do only the first few items and then they seem to begin missing the problems. After inspecting his work product, you realize that the problems on the bottom half of the page are equal in difficulty to the problems on the top half of the page. The point is that the student actually can do the problems; he just does not. Is there any magic in requiring that a student finish the complete page at one time? Try cutting the page in half or in fourths and letting the student do some activity between sections. He probably will complete all of the problems, and this is what you are after.

One viewpoint in education holds that students never make a wrong answer. What appears to be an error to the teacher is the result of a misunderstanding of the directions or of the question from the teacher.

One student was having a difficult time in learning the meaning of the modern math symbols "greater than" and "less than." The teacher decided to use different words to get the point across. Time after time the teacher indicated that 5 is less than 8; they are not the same; 8 is bigger than 5; etc. The student proved the teacher wrong by going to the board and measuring the numerals and indicated that they both were, in fact, equal because they were both three inches tall!! (Early, 1971).

Streff (1971) tells of the student who was consistently making "errors" on his subtraction facts; 5-3=5, 7-2=7, 9-4=9, etc. The teacher had marked all the answers wrong. However, when the student was asked to explain how he worked the problems, he responded that he did exactly what the teacher told the class to do. She had drawn five apples on the board and said, "Here we have five apples. You take away three, and what you have left is your answer." The student covered the 3 in the problem 5–3=5, and of course 5 was left on the board, so it was the answer.

Many times, in our ververbalization when we are teaching, we ask a question, continue talking, and then ask a question waiting for the answer from the student. When the student responds to the initial question, long forgotten by the teacher, his answer seems highly illogical or inappropriate at the time. We usually respond with some remark that does not enhance the self-concept of the student. How easy it would have been to ask, "How did you get the answer?" or "You've been thinking. Explain your answer to the class." This is a far cry from making the student feel in error by some comment that implies he is a poor student and consequently a less than worthwhile individual.

On an achievement test the following question is asked:

Apples are sold: (a)   by the quart
                        (b)   by the pound
                        (c)   by the yard
                        (d)   by the dozen

One boy marked letter (c) as the correct response. When questioned, he explained that he makes extra money for himself by picking apples off of the trees in his back yard and selling them to people out by the yard close to the street.

Most students do not interpret things in this "unusual" way, do they? No, they don't. But are those who do any less deserving of a few moments explanation of your instruction? Or an extra question to allow him to explain his answer? Whenever a student frowns or doesn't seem to understand what you are saying, before you consider that he is incapable of giving the correct answer, rethink your own instructions or directions. The true error might be on your part rather than his.

Communication with others, especially students, is not an easy task. What you say might not be exactly what you mean. A clever experiment is to take a set of geometric blocks; give someone else an identical set; put a barrier between you and the other person so that you cannot see what each is doing; build something and tell the other person the directions to build it, also. Then compare the product.

As teachers, we constantly run into situations which, in our opinion, require some modification of classroom behavior. Let's make it easy on ourselves, if that is possible. First look at our own verbalization, directions, and instructions. Look at the stimulus material. Possibly a change in these facets of instruction might be all that is needed.

SKETCHES OF BEHAVIOR MODIFICATION STUDIES

Grade or Age Level	Target Behavior	Methodology	Writers
Preschool (age 3.4)	Regressed crawling behavior	Adult attention given an immediate consequence.	Harris, et al. (1964)
Preschool (age 4)	Short attention span	Social reinforcement given to increase attention to a single task. Mother was powerful reinforcing figure.	Allen, et al. (1967)
Preschool	Climbing on playground equipment	Adult social reinforcement through successive approximations.	Johnston, et al. (1966)
TMR (ages 5 to 7)	Posture, awkwardness, fear of body movements	Points earned for distance crawled, walked, etc. Cookies and adult hugs and frolicking on gym mat. Increased mobility generalized to no fear of boarding school bus, gymnastics, etc.	Eposito (1970)
Grade 1	Inattention	Assigned an "office." Teacher ignored non-attending. Verbal praise given to the completion of each work assignment.	Morice (1968)
Grades 3 and 4 (remedial class)	Out-of-seat	Earned five points if in seat when buzzer sounded on the average of twenty minutes.	Wolf, et al. (1970)

SKETCHES OF BEHAVIOR MODIFICATION STUDIES

Grade or Age Level	Target Behavior	Methodology	Writers
Grade 1	Low work out-put, slowness	Color in a bar graph the number of the fifty problems finished in a work session each day, with praise given if the number correct increased over the prior day. Little increase. Teacher then gave the graph only if the number correct was equal to or greater than the prior day. Improvement noted.	McKenzie, et al. (1970)
Grade 1	Turning in Assignments	For each completed paper turned in, student received three minutes of mother's undivided attention. All assignments completed thereafter.	McKenzie, et al. (1970)
Grade 4	Disruptive Behavior	Teacher ignored outbursts, used self-reinforcement schedule of work assignments. Immediate verbal reinforcement given for completed assignments.	Morice (1968)
Grade 5 (age 11)	Interruptive behavior, arithmetic skills	Teacher ignored interruptive talking, attended only when student had permission. Correct arithmetic answers marked with "C," errors were ignored.	McKenzie, et al. (1970)

SKETCHES OF BEHAVIOR MODIFICATION STUDIES

Grade or Age Level	Target Behavior	Methodology	Writers
Grade 5	Teacher-dependent behavior, talk backs, throwing fits, verbal fighting	Use of time-out, sent home, points earned to trade for prizes.	Hardt (1971)
Grade 6	Low work out-put	Completed work earned points to exchange for money at home. This soon diminished. Student placed next to teacher and told he could return to his own desk when work was completed. Any time he had left over within the study time he could spend in his own way. Out-put increased because of his choice of free time activities.	Morice (1968)
Training School (ages 13 to 15)	Scores on test of TV news broadcasts, academic achievement	Use of token reinforcement redeemable for candy, chewing gum, etc.	Tyler and Brown (1968)
Junior High (ages 12 to 16)	Academic tasks	Points earned to trade for time at preferred activities. Chosen were handicrafts, typing, woodworking, organized games, and science units.	Nolen, et al. (1967)

CHAPTER V

Evaluating
Behavior

HOW IS YOUR project coming along? Is it working? How do you know?

To answer these questions you must somehow evaluate what you have done. You need information to help you decide if the project was successful. First, you might define what you mean by "successful." To one teacher it might mean one thing, to another, something else.

One approach to evaluating student behavior popular in education circles today is the use of behavioral or instructional objectives. This approach to evaluation essentially eliminates the use of complex statistical analysis. In establishing a behavior modification project, it might be wise to consider the use of behavioral objectives as you determine the design of your project. Self-instructional books on preparing objectives are available (Mager, 1962; Yellon and Scott, 1970).

To write a behavioral objective you should think of the behavior you want to see the student display. He is not doing it now, but if everything works out the way you want, he should be able to display the desired behavior. In other words, you are looking forward to the terminal behavior.

A properly written behavioral objective has several components. It tells:

1. under what circumstances

2. who
3. displays what behavior
4. how often

Let's say that a teacher has a problem with Billy who talks out and interrupts. The teacher wants him to learn to raise his hand for permission to speak. She has labeled the behavior she wants to increase and has defined it so that another observer would agree with her if the behavior occurred or did not occur. In addition she has determined the positive reinforcers to use and the schedule of reinforcement. She has collected baseline data on his hand-raising behavior for one week. She is ready to begin. But how does she know when to alter the reinforcement schedule from a continuous schedule to an intermittent schedule? In other words, how often does Billy have to raise his hand for the teacher to consider her project a success and for her to shift her project toward maintaining the new hand-raising behavior? So far, this has not been specified. A behavioral objective will help answer these questions.

Let's look at the components of an objective again and write a behavioral objective for the above situation. It might be something like this:

1. under what circumstances: Within the framework of the behavior
                              modification design
2. who   : Billy
3. displays what behavior : will raise his hand and not speak out
                              until recognized
4. how often   : during the discussion period in
                              Social Studies

A graph of the behavior might look something like this:

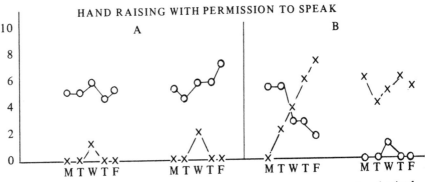

HAND RAISING WITH PERMISSION TO SPEAK

x = hand raised
o = talk outs

The teacher also wanted to tally the number of times Billy did talk out without raising his hand. These tallies are also shown. It seems that Billy makes about four or five comments each day. During baseline (A) his comments were often made without his hand raised and without permission. During (B) he gradually increased his hand raising, decreased the number of times he talked out, yet maintained his usual amount of classroom participation.

The teacher would probably consider that her objective had been attained by the end of (B). She would then switch to an intermittent reinforcement schedule to maintain his behavior.

Another objective might not require a 100 per cent level of performance. Such an objective might be:

> Within the behavior modification design specified, Susie will correctly name, with 90 per cent accuracy, the first twenty words of the basic word list when the teacher displays the words on the drill cards one at a time.

Once this objective is attained, the teacher would write a new objective to reflect the next higher level of instruction.

One teacher might be able to tolerate a certain level of behavior that another teacher would find completely unacceptable. If each of these two teachers had conducted a behavior modification project, each one would probably be satisfied with different levels of behavior as successful. For instance, if both teachers were modifying out-of-seat behavior and were using a ratio graph, one might define 20 per cent as an acceptable criterion level for success while the other teacher might require a 10 per cent level.

Having determined the criterion level of performance and having reached that level is one simple way to evaluate your project.

Another way to evaluate the effectiveness of a behavior modification project is to compare baseline data with data obtained after the project has begun. This can only be done if continuous recording of behavior takes place. The graphing of recording makes the comparison a simple task. This type of evaluation is generally called the ABAB design, or the reversal design. The baseline data is termed "A," and data during the management stage is termed "B." B is com-

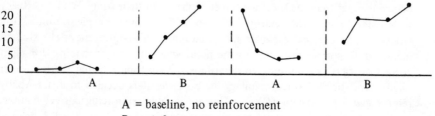

A = baseline, no reinforcement
B = reinforcement

pared with A to note any change. Then, the reinforcement program is terminated to revert to baseline conditions of A. The program is begun again and data for B is obtained. When the teacher sees the behavior graphed, she becomes aware of the high degree of influence she has on the student's behavior. She actually can arrange the environment in such a way that the student's behavior is modified. The ABAB design makes it very clear to her.

It stands to reason that conditions never can be identically similar to baseline. If a teacher initiates a behavior modification project, her attitude, general outlook, set, and expectancies do change. Returning to her behavior during baseline is practically impossible. The student's behavior also is altered. Behavior which was once reinforced probably has some different component than some similar behavior which has not been reinforced. Therefore, the ABAB design might best be called the ABA^1B^1 design to indicate the similarities *and* the differences.

In many instances when a teacher is learning about behavior modification, she collects baseline data while she is learning, such as you did. Inadvertently, she might have actually used some behavior modification techniques during that time. Altman and Linton (1971) suggested using an AABAB design incorporating two baselines, one before teacher training and one after teacher training. They noted that the "after teacher training" baseline might be more effective to use for a comparison with the baseline that is obtained after the first phase of modification is finished.

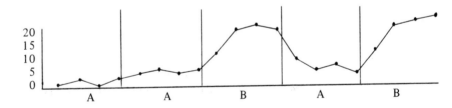

An approach to determine if the reinforcer used during a behavior modification project is a reliable reinforcer has been developed by Wolf and Risley (1967). In this approach the reinforcer is given when the student displays behavior other than the specified target behavior. In their study, Wolf and Risley were using food as the reinforcer for correctly naming the picture on a card. Gradually the correct responses increased under this contingency. The student increased his correct responses to the point where he was responding with eight correct answers per minute. To determine the contribution that the reinforcer might have for the correct naming, the experimenters decided to differentially reinforce *other* behavior (DRO). This meant *not* reinforcing correct naming. Under this contingency the correct naming dropped to a zero level. Later the earlier procedure, in which correct naming only was reinforced, was employed.

The rate quickly returned to approximately the previous level. It was concluded that the reinforcer of food could account for the correct naming.

A graph might look like this:

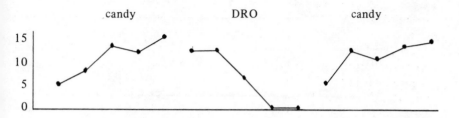

A similar technique is not without possibility in the classroom. To determine if a particular reinforcer "works," use it to reinforce a different behavior. If the different behavior is increased, you can be rather certain that the reinforcer is meaningful.

The ABAB design is sometimes called the "reverse" design. Another design used for evaluation is called the multiple baseline design. The techniques of the design are used to establish scientific verification of the procedures in order to determine if the procedures were responsible for the changes in behavior which were observed (Hall and others 1970).

Hall and others (1970) reported on three types of multiple baseline designs suggested by Risley and Baer (in press) which were conducted by teachers and parents. One type of multiple baseline involved two or more behaviors on the same individual. The experimental procedure is introduced to one of the behaviors, then to the other. The purpose of this approach is to determine if the experimental procedure actually caused the change in behavior. If the behavior actually changes when the experimental procedures are applied and no change is observed prior to the procedures, then it is inferred that a causal relationship exists.

If a teacher wanted to observe behaviors X and Y on Susie and the experimental procedures might be labeled P, the behaviors X and Y would first be graphed. The experimental procedures P would be applied to X, then later to Y. The observation would be maintained throughout the project and charted. The results might look something like the chart at the top of page 78.

The experimental procedures P were applied to behavior X on the sixth day and the behavior improved. The procedures were not applied to behavior Y until the ninth day. Behavior Y was maintained at a low level until the procedures were applied to it even though behavior X and the procedures were in effect. It was assumed that the procedures actually caused the improvement in behavior X and later in behavior Y.

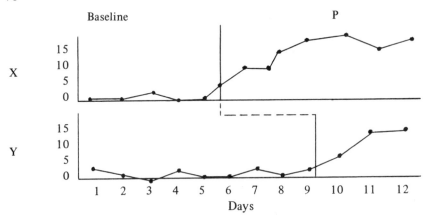

A second type of baseline involves measuring the same behavior of different students in the same situation. After baseline data are graphed, the experimental procedures are applied to one of the students, then to the other, and so on. If changes are noted, it can be assumed that the behaviors of the students are contingent upon the procedures that are used. The procedure is similar to the previously mentioned baseline. A graph might look like this:

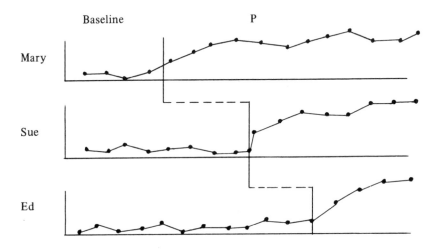

Obviously, the procedures were related to an increase of the same behavior for the three students.

The third type of baseline involves observing the same behavior in one student in differing situations. Hall and others (1970) gave examples of these designs.

In evaluating the projects we need to be sure that the behaviors measured are in fact stable (reliable) behaviors. Reliability checks can be obtained by having another observer also tally the behavior which you are observing and then determining the percentage of agreement. Hall (1971a) discussed a technique to determine reliability between observers. When working with tallying the number of times a student displays a particular behavior, the lowest number tallied by one observer is divided by the highest number tallied by the other observer. The answer is multiplied by 100 to obtain the percentage of agreement.

If you observed Johnny raise his hand ten times during the math lesson while your teacher friend observed him twelve times, the percentage of agreement would be 83.3 per cent (10 ÷ 12 X 100 = 83.3%). Usually we strive for at least 90 per cent agreement.

RESEARCH DESIGNS AND ANALYSIS

Usually the success of a project is determined through properly designed and analyzed research techniques. Such techniques have been discussed in the now classic chapter by Campbell and Stanley (1963). They view educational research as an approach to control for internal and external validity, citing factors which might jeopardize such validity. In addition, they give examples of pre-experimental designs, true experimental designs, and quasi-experimental designs and discuss appropriate analysis of them.

While most educational research is concerned with a comparison between an experimental group and a control group, in behavior modification we are primarily concerned with repeated measures on one individual. The research design of interest to us is typically called repeated-measures design, or time-series design. This design is used in longitudinal studies of students over a period of time.

Such designs are not without their troublesome aspects. In discussing these areas of caution, Campbell and Stanley (1963) suggest that some explanation other than the experimental treatment (in our case, reinforcement) might account for the change of behavior noted. This is highly probable in situations such as the classroom where all sorts of things are going on; it is less likely in a laboratory situation where the many possible variables are accounted for. When events in the environment other than the experimental treatment are contributory to the change in behavior, the source of invalidity is called *history*. In order to be assured that the effects of history are not contributing to behavior change, the project should be conducted long enough, over enough days, to take into consideration any possible effects due to an approaching grading period, parent visitation night, vacations, special PTA programs, or what have you.

Kerlinger (1965) also commented on the effects of history in a longitudinal time design. If the observations on an individual are illustrated by Y and the beginning of a behavior modification project illustrated by X:

$$Y_1 \quad Y_2 \quad X \quad Y_3 \quad Y_4$$

then the research design is similar to Kerlinger's design 17.8 (p. 318):

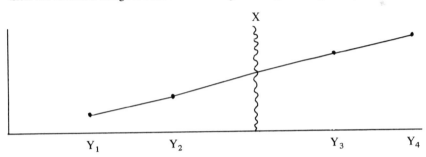

If the design had used only one observation before the experimental procedure and only one observation after it, design Y_1 X Y_2 and if the difference between the observations were determined to be of significance, "one cannot tell whether X or a time variable caused the change. But with design 17.8, one has other measures of Y and thus a baseline against which to compare the change in Y presumably due to X" (Kerlinger, 1965, p. 317). The use of many observations helps determine if history might in fact account for the change in behavior. These events would occur between Y_1, and Y_2, between Y_2 and Y_3, and between Y_3 and Y_4. We would be able to see, if the observations were graphed, the pattern of behavior prior to X and after X. These graphed observations would help us decide the effectiveness of X and any effects of history. We need to ask if there might have been anything other than the experimental procedure that might account for any difference between Y_2 and Y_3.

If we generalize these comments to our previous discussion, we can see the similarity if we consider that several observations, Ys, occur within the period of observation labeled as A and B thusly:

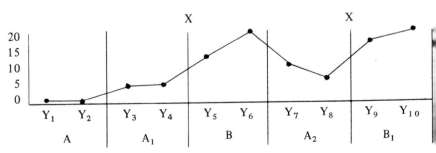

where

A   = baseline prior to teacher training
A_1 = baseline during teacher training
B   = reinforcement in effect for target behavior
A_2 = reverting to no reinforcement for target behavior
B_1 = reinstigation of reinforcement for target behavior

Behavior modification projects have more than two observations during A, A_1, etc., since the baseline period usually lasts for several days.

Because you have graphed your observations, you are able to determine if the change might be a simple result of *maturation* since you can show if any gradual change over time has occurred.

In some experiments, students are tested one or more times for the purpose of gathering data or assessing the results of the experiment. The effects that taking the first test have on the second test might account for possible higher scores on the second test. The students are primed, or they have psyched out what the examiner wants. If you had considered using a pre- and post-test in your project, you should be cautiously aware of the influence it might have. Such caution is of special importance when you are not dealing with two or more groups. Again, your longitudinal observations help you to judge if these effects occurred.

Another source of invalidity is *instrumentation,* those changes in the measuring instrument or observation which might attribute to the behavior change. If you have labeled the behavior and defined it in such a way that two or more people will consistently agree that it has or has not occurred, this source of invalidity does not exist for behavior modification studies, even when the person doing the observation or tallying of behavior is someone other than you.

Other sources, *regression effects* and *selection,* are ruled out as possible sources of invalidity because of the length of time of your project and because you are observing the same individual throughout. Likewise, *mortality,* the loss of subjects, is not likely to be a problem in behavior modification. If mortality does occur, your project is ended anyway.

In regard to external validity, the generalization of results to situations not within your present study, behavior modification studies with individuals pose more of a problem than studies using groups. Individuals are probably more unique than groups. What works for Johnny might not work for Harry. But, if it did work for Johnny, you could determine if it would work for Harry, then for Tommy, then George, etc. After several trials you could establish a probability of success for a particular project. Not only would you be concerned about some specific component of the project, say some special approach to positive rein-forcement, but you could also be concerned about the generalization of the theoretical framework of behavior modification to other, possibly more varied, situations.

Most educational research analyzes the results of a project to determine if the results are statistically significant. This is usually done by comparing the average score of the experimental group with the average score of a non-experimental, or control, group. When we are conducting essentially a longitudinal time design with many observations, statistical analysis of the observations to determine significance of change poses problems. Some problems in such analysis mentioned by Kerlinger (1965) were (a) spurious results of significance tests, (b) high variability of time data, and (c) observed change being interpreted as expected change. He suggested that such analyses be confined to graphs to show the results and to interpret the results qualitatively. If more complex statistical interpretation is desired, and such interpretations should be sought for a more rigorous scientific inquiry, a statistician and an educational research specialist should be consulted.

For a review of research methodology and statistical analysis, Parton and Ross (1965) offered a detailed review of studies using social reinforcement for a simple motor task of placing marbles in a hole. They suggested that research in this area needs to indicate greater reliability of the reinforcement through repeated measures of baseline and reinforcement performance. Most studies used only one estimation of performance at each stage, thereby rendering the stability of the performance questionable.

A highly sophisticated analysis of charted results of a behavior modification project might be accomplished by trend analysis. However, the design of the project should be such that the observations and reinforcement procedures meet the requirements of such analysis.

Hall (1971b) has compared the new approach to measurement and research which consists of graphing data with the more traditional statistical analysis approach. Paul (1969) has reviewed several designs and tactics in evaluating behavior modification projects.

CRITICISM OF BEHAVIOR MODIFICATION

The field of behavior modification and of behavior therapy is not viewed by everyone as a bed of roses. Many criticisms come from a misunderstanding of the theory; some come from an honest belief that other theories are better. MacMillan and Forness (1970) cautioned against viewing it as a panacea since other theorists can also adequately explain behavior. An awareness, and, consequently, a position for debate, has reached the national political level where the concern is the perpetuation of individualization (Agnew, 1972; Goodall, 1972).

In discussing the behavior model Arthur (1969) summarized the comments of the critics. According to the critics, behavior therapy does not deal with the abstractions of life such as aspirations, hopes, needs, disappointments, etc. Other approaches to behavior change might be more efficient and might reflect change through insight, growth, etc. The direction in therapy might not be towards a societal norm. The therapists should be clinical personnel, without whom the model cannot be used.

Stuart (1970) also summarized the responses of critics. Highly criticized are research designs by those who support an opposing theory which is even less verified. Other critics have attacked the basic tenets of behavioral therapy because other tenets oppose the medical model. Reactions to the criticism attempt to countermand and allay those concerns. In response to situations indicating failure of a behavior modification project, Stuart cautioned that when the design is to decrease responses prior to increasing adaptive responses, a source of reinforcement has been withdrawn and the reinforcement is sought out through an alternative maladaptive behavior.

Three negative effects resulting from exclusive training in the "learning theory" school were mentioned by Portes (1971). These were (1) other explanations can account for behavior, (2) the patient might be aware of the problem, and his reaction to his awareness might affect his behavior, and (3) the objective manner of the patient-therapist relationship might result in less caring for the person. He builds a case for the existence of a "self-awareness" by attributing it as the cause for both positive and negative generalization of one behavior to other behaviors, as the cause for the success of social reinforcement, and as an explanation for why individuals can participate in their own conditioning program. Eysenck (1971) published a scholarly rebuttal to Portes's criticism, pointing out that to approach the field scientifically present theories must face oversimplification. He also noted that the theory should be judged in terms of its successes and failures in relationship to its aims and that the data give support to the direction in which behavior therapy is moving.

Stott (1971) in more of a caution than a criticism reminded us that most students also learn from disapproval expressed by parents, teachers, and peers. Most citizens require restraints and when these are removed socially undesirable behavior might be manifest. He mentioned that "when tempted to indulge in disruptive behavior the normal child desists therefrom when faced with the disapproval of the teachers or his classmates. And the fear of disapproval is stronger, let us repeat, for the normal child, than the notoriety gained by bad behavior." Essentially this point was raised previously when we discussed the effects of avoidance when faced with a punitive situation or person.

Another criticism relates to the cold and noncaring tone that exists within behavior modification. Ross (1967) remarked that "behavior therapy is sometimes accused of being impersonal, mechanical, manipulative, and authoritarian.

Some of this is no doubt due to the rather unfortunate terminology that derives from the psychological laboratory. Words like 'control,' 'contingency,' 'schedule,' 'program,' and 'conditioning' do indeed sound prohibitive, but as soon as one substitutes 'learning' for 'conditioning,' 'planning' for 'programming,' 'handling' for 'control,' one finds that the concepts as such are not at all objectionable.''

For those critics who feel that the teacher is a cold impersonal manipulator, Ross went on to point out that behavior therapy does things *for* people, not *to* people. The student actually carries out his own treatment or learning and the procedure is based on his needs, not those of the teacher. The process is clearly explained to the student and based on observable and measurable events so that both the student and the teacher can see the progress or the lack of it. Nothing is based on the authority of the teacher or on faith, as in other approaches.

In discussing the moral issues in behavior modification, London (1970, p. 187) remarked that the control that a teacher might have is more than a practical matter, "but a moral imperative which he must fulfill in order to maintain his right to offer help at all."

When it is realized that the teacher is quite capable of altering behavior of students, the desired behavior must be judged as having some value and worth. Birnbrauer, Jurchard, and Burchard (1970, p. 22) ask, "Will modification of the behavior enable the individual to adapt more effectively to his environment and how can the occurrence of the behavior be reliably recorded? By adapting effectively we mean developing behavior that conforms to laws and social mores and also leads to greater self-sufficiency." They suggest that the basis of selecting the desired behavior might rest on what the student will need in order to live productively, to be sociable and acceptable, and to continue to develop.

To this writer it appears that the trend in most criticisms of behavior modification is that it does not recognize the feelings of either the student or the teacher and that it does not account for self-directed behavior on the part of the student as typically and traditionally expressed in the terminology of self-awareness, ego strength, values, needs, aims, goals, satisfaction, etc.

These concerns might be understood at this point in our society which is experiencing the throes of sociological change. Most of the reported studies in behavior modification deal with structured behaviors (in-seat, talk-outs, disruptive activity, aggressiveness, temper tantrums, etc.). The critics might say that the behaviors are interpreted by the teacher as disruptive while the intent of the student is "self-expression." If teachers stifle behaviors through manipulation, we are creating a world of expressionless non-persons.

There are those who would argue that the attainment of skills is a minor goal for education. More important is understanding self and having a sensitivity to others so that better interpersonal relationships can develop. For some students these things must be learned. If a behavior such as "having a sensitivity to the feelings of others" can be defined, then it can be taught with the principles of behavior modification.

Rogers (1969) viewed the teacher as a facilitator of learning. He felt that behavior does change when an individual chooses to be free.

One of man's goals is freedom to think and to act for himself within the laws and mores of our changing society. When he does this successfully, he feels a sense of pride and achievement. He finds energy to try new things, to experiment, to grow. He is creative and offers the results of his creativity to others so that they might also sense a feeling of joy and happiness. The world looks bright and extremely worthwhile.

A different world might exist if every student from preschool through adult education would have such a viewpoint about himself, about life, and about education. Some students do; others do some of the time; yet there are those whose entire educational experience seems filled almost totally with despair. It is probably for this last group that behavior modification can be of most value in helping them learn that their way of life can become personally rewarding.

Many so-called emotionally disturbed children are under treatment at an early school age. Life for them is certainly neither free nor rewarding. Sometimes we see a glimmer of hope when the student says, "But, Teacher! I'd rather do it myself!" We are hoping that internal reinforcement becomes powerful enough so that when a task is performed, the student beams with self-pride. For these children, it might be that teachers should plan to give external social reinforcement when such pride is displayed. It might be that a more specified arrangement of reinforcement from concrete tangibles to social reinforcement and ultimately to self-reinforcement would bring about such a desired sense of freedom.

Some of the critics of behavior modification might have said, "But I want the student to develop a good self-concept." "Self-concept" is in itself an abstract concept. It might be defined by a score on a certain projective-type test. You might define it by saying a student with a good self-concept feels that he can succeed in school, has lots of friends, and is happy. We can measure these traits if they are defined, but do the results show us a self-concept?

Other teachers, say, "I want the students to have a good *attitude* toward school." Attitudes, like self-concepts, are not directly observable. Our problem is that we are talking in non-behavioral terms. You cannot *see* an attitude or a self-concept, yet somehow you "know" the students have them. What you *can* do is *see* the behavior that a student displays and thereby *infer* a certain attitude or self-concept.

When a student consistently says, "I can't," "Nobody likes me," etc., we infer that he has a poor self-concept. You want to change it. Or you might want to change the student's attitude. The same principle applies here, too. You must observe what the student does before you can infer what attitude he has. If we think of behavior rather than "self-concept" or "attitude" or any other of the many abstract terms found in education, we should be able to plan the environment so that positive conditions and positive responses occur to the extent that the new behaviors would lead the teacher to remark on the goodness of the self-concept and attitude. Mager (1968) has an excellent paperback addressed to this subject.

The technique and theory of behavior modification should be able to assist teachers in developing these desired behaviors. Kroth (1968) has used the Q-Sort technique of assessing "self-concept" changes as a result of behavior modification programming. The student sorts out statements into those that describe him now and those that describe how he would like to be. These give the teacher an idea of contingencies to arrange to bring into line any discrepancy reported by the student. At the end of a behavior modification program the student sorts the statements again and the teacher can determine if the program has had an effect on the descriptions reported by the student. It seems that a more positive self-concept can be molded through behavior modification.

Behavior changes in elementary school children were observed by Harris (1969) when the parents served as models to them. The children saw how their parents communicated using the P-A-C (Parent, Adult, Child) technique. Changes in the parents' behavior occurred when they learned to "free up their Adult" in their transactions with others. This approach can also be used with the students.

The contract system was mentioned by Harris as an effective approach which assured consistency in direction and discipline. Adherence to the contract brings meaningful reinforcement to the student both externally (he gets something for filling it) and internally (he feels good about himself).

The P-A-C approach appears to have promise in ensuring that communication occurs among people, such as between the teacher and the students in school. Reinforcement might assist the learning of the method in students. When the teacher does give a reward to a student, if it is given from the teacher's Adult to the student's Adult, chances are that it will be perceived as a worthwhile and meaningful act on the part of the teacher and not one of false innuendoes.

CLOSING COMMENT

Since we know that the skills of teachers can selectively influence the way a student behaves, these skills should be used as the teacher considers developing behaviors other than simply staying in the seat, the number of math problems correctly completed, raising of hands, etc. These structured behaviors are necessary only with certain students in certain situations in order to allow the student to move toward learning those behaviors which bring an ever increasing number and amount of intrinsic reinforcement and social reinforcement for pro-self/social behaviors. These new behaviors are typically referred to as good self-concept, awareness of self and others, social graces, a concern for one's fellow man, having a cause bigger than one's self, etc.

While many students seem to build behavior in this direction in spite of what goes on in the classroom, and while many teachers seem to "naturally" create an environment in which these behaviors easily develop, it is for those teachers who have expressed a concern for a methodology to create this environment that the techniques of behavior modification might be of real benefit.

The first step toward such a goal is for the teacher to sense himself as a person who *can* provide such an environment. Having used the techniques in this book, many teachers report that since they have been positively reinforced for molding appropriate student behavior, their outlook on life and on their job is more positive.

This is a good beginning – now let's continue with the tasks to be done.

Notes from the Cum Folder

Name   Charlie
CA   9-4
Grade   4
Parents   Mr. and Mrs. F. Jones
          Occupation of Father — lineman, telephone company
          Occupation of Mother — housewife
Siblings Jack, age 13, grade 8
          Mary, age 3

TEACHER COMMENTS

Kindergarten:

Charlie is a small boy for his age. He seems to have acquired most of the readiness skills to prepare him for first grade next year, but he is quite an immature youngster. He gets along well with the other children until they do not go along with him. He has had two rather bad tantrums this second semester. There are days that he is more interested in playing by himself with the blocks than participating in the group math lessons. Most of the time he is a pleasant child. I do not think he is ready for the first grade socially. He will find the pace of the curriculum quite fast for him. I am recommending another year of Kindergarten because of his immaturity.

NOTE: Mrs. Jones came in for a parent conference at my request. The principal and I suggested that we let Charlie repeat Kindergarten for another year. She said that she would discuss it with her husband and let us know. Mrs. Jones appeared to be quite surprised at our recommendation, saying that she thought Charlie was doing as well as the other children.

NOTE: Dear Mrs. Jackson: My wife and I have discussed what you said about keeping Charlie back next year. I think Charlie is a good boy and learns OK. I don't want him to take Kindergarten next year. He should be in the first grade with his friends. If he fails the first grade, then we'll see. Sincerely, Mr. F. Jones.

NOTE: Since it is school policy not to retain students against the wishes of the parents, Charlie was advanced, not promoted, to first grade.

First Grade:

Charlie did just enough work to get by. I gave him the benefit of the doubt, hoping to motivate him to do more work. The readiness test at the beginning of the year indicated a 48 percentile score which suggests low average ability, but his work has not reflected that ability. He is a slow mover, I am passing him on to the second grade hoping that the teacher can motivate him better than I did.

Second Grade:

Charlie has intellectual capabilities to do better work than he does. He makes a "C" on the work that he turns in, which is seldom. He loves to play rough on the playground and has been in a few fights. I wish he would put some of that energy into learning to read. He is in the bottom reading group. He was out of school two weeks with a cold and missed our reading tests. While he acquires math concepts quickly, he is simply not interested in doing the work. He would rather roam about the room or play with the toy cars.

Third Grade:

I called Charlie's parents in for a conference because he does not turn in his papers. Mr. Jones did not come, but Mrs. Jones did. She seems interested in Charlie, but she does not appear to be the type who can do much about making him study. She mentioned that her new baby is keeping her busy. She will talk to her husband, and they will see what they can do.

I asked the school psychologist to test Charlie. He has average ability (IQ 105) which is higher than some of the other students in my class. On his achievement test, he achieved grade equivalent scores of 3.2 in arithmetic and 3.4 in reading comprehension. These scores are higher than what his classroom performance would suggest. He wastes time, yet he does not cause a disturbance. I moved him up into the middle reading group at the end of the year and he showed improvement for a while. Failure would be inadvisable, but the fourth grade will be difficult for him.

Fourth Grade:

I thought I would add this note to the cum folder before first semester grades came out. Charlie's popularity certainly increased this year. He is really a very likable boy and enjoys school. He is in the second reading group and does an average job. But, he does *not* do any work in the math lessons. We changed texts this year, but the content is not much different from what it was last year (both texts were modern math).

Just to indicate how much, or how little, he does during math, I kept a record of the number of problems he did for two weeks. The new workbooks are set up for this unit so that there are twenty problems on each page. I give the class time to do the work, and they turn in the page at the end of the day.

	number of problems answered	number of correct answers
M	5	4
T	4	4
W	10	8
Th	7	5
F	6	5
M	3	3
T	7	5
W	17	12
Th	5	4
F	8	6

Charlie usually gets most of what he does correct. His mistakes are usually silly errors. He could get all of the problems correct if he would only try. We had a movie each Wednesday and the class had to get its work done in the morning. He worked more on those days than on the other days. He wastes so much time in the back of the room. I purchased some puzzles with the PTA money, and they are kept on a table for the students to work when they have finished their assignments. Charlie manages to find himself back there playing with the puzzles instead of doing his work. When I tell him to sit down and work, he will do so, but he's back at that table again in three minutes. I don't want to give him a D in math, but his daily grades are so low that I'm afraid that is what he will earn. I *know* he can do better!

NOTES BY AN OBSERVER IN CHARLIE'S CLASSROOM

When I walked in Charlie's room, it looked like most other fourth grade classrooms. There were approximately thirty students in the room. Miss Stanford, Charlie's teacher, had a large table in each of the two far corners. There were two other smaller tables along the side of the room each seating four or five students. There were three rows of six desks arranged horizontally in front of the teacher's desk toward the front of the room.

Along one side of the room were shelves and bookcases. In these were textbooks and other reading materials. On the shelves were an aquarium, a gerbil, a terrarium, and a mysterious pile of seemingly useless junk consisting of crushed cans, balls of string, old newspapers, a broken tennis racket, and other odds and ends all thrown together into a big box.

Some of the art supplies were located in cabinets on the far side of the room. They were behind the desks used for small group work. All of the other more essential supplies and materials were readily available on the open shelves on the opposite side of the room.

Some students were at the two tables working in small groups. At one of the tables a sixth grader was working with three boys on some math drill. Charlie was one of the three boys. He was working well and all of the students seemed to be having a good time learning. At one point when the boys were laughing at some obvious mistake that one of the students had made, Miss Stanford ignored the situation as did the other students.

There were five students working independently at various locations around the room. One was working on math worksheets, two were reading a book, one was looking at a filmstrip on vowel sounds, and one boy was rummaging through the junk box. The remaining students were sitting with the teacher for a group lesson. The teacher's questions facilitated reasoning as well as the learning of math concepts. Most of the students were paying attention. Two students appeared not interested in the presentation. One student's attention was drawn to the junk box and the other student was daydreaming. Miss Stanford did not call attention to either of the students during her presentation.

During the group lesson some of the other students went over to look at the aquarium for a few minutes. They eventually returned to their seatwork. One of the students in the group quietly left the room. Miss Stanford saw him leave and made no comment about it.

The atmosphere in Miss Stanford's room appears to be relaxed with a minimal amount of structure.

Charlie's Teacher

Miss Stanford has been teaching for three years. She attends the local state university and is taking classes in the evening expecting to finish her master's degree at the end of the summer term. Even though her major is in elementary education, her interests are in the areas of counselling, educational psychology, and innovative curricula. The master's degree is viewed as an obstacle to overcome solely because of the state requirement. She does not consider herself a "professional" student and is not considering advanced work for a specialist or doctorate degree. However, she is quite interested in attending inservice workshops offered for teachers in her school system. After completion of the master's degree, Miss Stanford plans to simply take some courses of interest to her such as anthropology or weaving. She is generally dissatisfied with the content and quality of the courses offered in teacher training at the university and feels that inservice training for practicing teachers would be valuable.

Miss Stanford lives with her roommate who is employed as a legal secretary. Her best friend at school is Sara Johnson, a sixth grade teacher with 20 years teaching experience. Sara and Miss Stanford teach in the same wing of the building and see each other frequently in the hall. Since all of the students eat lunch at the same hour, they typically spend their lunch hour together. They try to get out of the building every Friday to cash their checks and to grab a bite at a local restaurant. At one time last year, Miss Stanford and Sara had a serious disagreement and their relationship was strained for several days. They agreed to get together after school and discuss their differences. Miss Stanford recalled her exposure to transactional analysis in one of her educational psychology classes and explained the approach to Sara. Both of them agreed that it would appear to be promising for them to use in their communication with each other. Since that time they have attempted to speak frankly on subjects they disagree about and to accept the other's opinion in a non-threatening way.

Miss Stanford relates well with other staff members. She rarely has an opportunity to talk to teachers in the primary wing, but she is accepted as a "veteran" staff member. The turnover in her school averages two teachers yearly.

At the beginning of this year, Miss Stanford and the other teachers in her wing decided to meet after school to discuss the concept of team teaching. They wondered if this approach would be of benefit to their students. This meeting was instigated by one of the more traditional fifth grade teachers. These meetings are now in progress. The teachers meet once a week and have a local university professor consulting with them. They have visited another school in the system, which is highly individualized, to learn about that approach. Miss Stanford has attempted some individualization within her self-contained classroom and feels satisfied with the progress.

The experience range varies from first year teachers to two members who will be retiring at the end of this school year. The new teachers are equally divided between primary and elementary grades.

The school is fortunate to have a small teacher's lounge for coffee and conversation. Rarely does the conversation in the lounge center around "professional" topics. Miss Stanford attributes this to the fact that the teachers like to take their minds off of their job while in the lounge. Politics is a perennial topic as well as local school board actions, flat tires, and golf scores.

Miss Stanford's opinion of the school principal is expressed in a matter-of-fact way. Since he is new this year, no one knows him well. He was transferred from a sixth grade teaching position in another school where he served as a part-time assistant principal. He attempts to be fair in dealing with both staff and students. He is relatively a young man and is cognizant of the new educational approaches. The staff feels, however, that while he is familiar with these approaches, he personally tends to be more traditional. While he does not implement new ideas solely for the sake of change, he has allowed staff members to attempt new programs on a trial basis.

All in all, Charlie's school might be considered a typical school.

References

Agnew, S.T. Address given to the Farm Bureau. *Psychology Today,* January 1972, p. 4.

Allen, K.E., Henke, L.B., Harris, F.R., Baer, D.M., and Reynolds, N.J. "Control of Hyperactivity by Social Reinforcement of Attending Behavior." *Journal of Educational Psychology.* 58 (1967): 231-237.

Allen, K.E., Turner, K.D., and Everett, P.M. "A Behavior Modification Classroom for Head Start Children with Problem Behaviors." *Exceptional Children* 37 (1970: 119-127.

Altman, K.I., and Linton, T.E. "Operant Conditioning in the Classroom Setting: A Review of the Research." *Journal of Educational Psychology* 64 (1971): 277-286.

Ames, L.B. "A Low Intelligence Quotient Often Not Recognized as the Chief Cause of Many Learning Difficulties." *Journal of Learning Disabilities* 1 (1968): 735-739.

Arthur, A.Z. "Diagnostic Testing and the New Alternatives." *Psychological Bulletin* 72 (1969): 183-192.

Becker, W.C. *Parents Are Teachers.* Champaign, Ill.: Research Press, 1971.

Becker, W.C., Thomas, D.R., and Carnine, D. *Reducing Behavior Problems: An Operant Conditioning Guide for Teachers.* Urbana,: ERIC, 1969.

Berelson, B., and Steiner, G.A. *Human Behavior.* New York: Harcourt, Brace & World, 1964.

Bijou, S.W. "Experimental Studies of Child Behavior, Normal and Deviant." In *Research in Behavior Modification,* edited by L. Krasner and L.P. Ullmann. New York: Holt, Rinehart & Winston, 1965.

Bijou, S.W., and Baer, D.M. *Child Development.* New York: Appleton-Century-Crofts, 1961.

Birnbrauer, J.S., Jurchard, J.D., and Burchard, S.N. "Wanted: Behavior Analysts." In *Behavior Modification: The Human Effort,* edited by R.H. Bradfield. San Rafael: Dimensions Publishing, 1970.

Bricker, W.A. "Principles of Behavior Modification." In *Cumberland House Studies in Behavior Modification,* edited by D.D. Bricker. Nashville: Tennessee Re-Education Center, (no date).

Brophy, J.E., and Good, T.L. "Teacher's Communication of Differential Expectations for Children's Classroom Performance: Some Behavioral Data." *Journal of Educational Psychology* 61 (1970): 365-374.

Campbell, D.T., and Stanley, J.E. "Experimental and Quasi-Experimental Designs for Research on Teaching." In *Handbook of Research on Teaching,* edited by N.L. Gage, pp. 171-246. New York: Rand McNally, 1963.

Chaffin, J., and Kroth, R. Workshop on Behavior Modification. Hammond, Ind., March 1971.

Clarizio, H.F., and Yellon, S.L. "Learning Theory Approaches to Classroom Management: Rationale and Intervention Techniques." *Journal of Special Education* 1 (1967): 267-274.

Curry, D.R. "Case Studies in Behavior Modification." *Psychology in the Schools* 7 (1970): 330-335.

Early, F. Workshop on Perceptual-motor Development presented at the Diagnostic Teaching Center, Indianapolis Public Schools, Indianapolis, Ind., September 1971.

Esposito, F.G. "Premack's Principle Applied to Retarded Preschool Children." *Experimental Publication System,* October 1970, 8, Ms. No. 287-3.

Eysenck, H.J. "Behavior Therapy as a Scientific Discipline." *Journal of Consulting and Clinical Psychology* 36 (1971): 314-319.

Fox, L. "Effecting the Use of Efficient Study Habits." In *Control of Human Behavior,* edited by R. Ulrich, T. Stachnik, and J. Mabry. Glenview, Ill.: Scott, Foresman, 1966.

Gaasholt, M. "Precision Teaching in the Management of Teacher and Child Behavior." *Exceptional Children.* 37 (1970): 129-135.

Gagne, R.M. *The Conditions of Learning.* New York: Holt, Rinehart & Winston, 1965.

Gelfand, D.M., and Hartmann, D.P. "Behavior Therapy with Children: A Review and Evaluation of Research Methodology." *Psychological Bulletin* 69 (1968): 204-215.

Glavin, J.P., Quay, H.C., and Werry, J.S. "Behavioral and Academic Gains of Conduct Problem Children in Different Classroom Settings." *Exceptional Children* 37 (1971): 441-446.

Goodall, K. "Tie Line." *Psychology Today.* January 1972, p. 24.

Hall, R.V. *Managing Behavior. Behavior Modification: The Measurement of Behavior.* Lawrence, Kan.: H & H Enterprises, Inc., 1971a.

Hall, R.V. "Responsive Teaching: Focus on Measurement and Research in the Classroom and the Home." *Focus on Exceptional Children* 3 (December 1971b): 1-7.

Hall, R.V., Cristler, C., Cranston, S.S., and Tucker, B. "Teachers and Parents as Researchers Using Multiple Baseline Designs." *Journal of Applied Behavior Analysis* 3 (1970): 247-255.

Hardt, F.A. "Modification of a Temper Tantrum." *Experimental Publication System*, February 1971, 10, Ms. No. 383-35.

Harris, F.R., Johnston, M.K., Kelley, C.S., and Wolf, M.M. "Effects of Positive Social Reinforcement on Regressed Crawling of a Nursery School Child." *Journal of Educational Psychology* 55 (1964): 35-41.

Harris, T.A. *I'm OK – You're OK.* New York: Harper & Row, 1969.

Holgate, S.H. "Operant Principles and the Emotionally Disturbed Child." *Experimental Publication System*, April 1971, 11, Ms. No. 436-34.

Holmes, D.S. "The Application of Learning Theory to the Treatment of a School Behavior Problem: A Case Study." *Psychology in the School* 3 (1966): 354-359.

Homme, L.W. "Contingency Management." In Newsletter of the American Psychological Association Division of Clinical Psychology, Section on Clinical Child Psychology, edited by M.R. Cluck. 1966, 5, No. 4, November.

Ilg, F.L., and Ames, L.B. *School Readiness.* New York: Harper & Row, 1964.

Johnston, M.K., Kelley, C.S., Harris, F.R., and Wolf, M.M. "An Application of Reinforcement Principles to Development of Motor Skills of a Young Child." *Child Development* 37 (1966): 379-387.

Karnes, M.B. *Helping Young Children Develop Language Skills: A Book of Activities.* Washington, D.C.: CEC, 1968.

Keller, F.S. *Learning – Reinforcement Theory.* New York: Random House, 1954.

Kephart, N.C. *The Slow Learner in the Classroom.* Columbus, Ohio: Charles E. Merrill Publishers, Second Edition, 1971.

Kerlinger, F.N. *Foundations of Behavioral Research.* New York: Holt, Rinehart & Winston, 1965.

Kirk, S.A., McCarthy, J.J., and Kirk, W.D. *Illinois Test of Psycholinguistic Abilities (rev. ed.).* Champaign, Ill.: University of Illinois Press, 1968.

Krasner, L., and Ullmann, L.P. *Research in Behavior Modification.* New York: Holt, Rinehart & Winston, 1965.

Kroth, R. *The Behavioral Q-Sort as a Diagnostic Instrument.* University of Kansas, 1968. Mimeographed.

Kroth, R. Workshop on Behavior Modification. Presented to school psychologists in Indiana. Indiana University Medical Center, Indianapolis, November, 1970.

Krumboltz, J.D. "Promoting Adaptive Behavior: New Answers to Familiar Questions. In *Revolution in Counseling,* edited by J. D. Krumboltz. Boston: Houghton Mifflin, 1966. Cited in Arthur, A.Z. "Diagnostic Testing and the New Alternative." *Psychological Bulletin* 72 (1969): 183-192.

Lang, P.J. "The Mechanics of Desensitization and the Laboratory Study of Human Fear." In *Behavior Therapy: Appraisal and Status,* edited by C.M. Franks. New York: McGraw-Hill, 1969. Cited by M. Whitman and J. Whitman, "Behavior Modification in the Classroom." *Psychology in the Schools* 8 (1971): 176-186.

London, P. "Moral Issues in Behavior Modification." In *Behavior Modification: The Human Effort*, edited by R.H. Bradfield. San Rafael, Calif.: Dimensions Publishing Co., 1970.

Lovitt, T. "Behavior Modification: The Current Scene." *Exceptional Children* 37 (1970): 85-91.

MacMillan, D.L., and Forness, S.R. "Behavior Modification: Limitations and Liabilities." *Exceptional Children* 37 (1970): 291-297.

Mager, R.F. *Preparing Instructional Objectives.* Palo Alto: Fearon Publishers, 1962.

Mager, R.F. *Developing Attitude Toward Learning.* Palo Alto: Fearon Publishers, 1968.

McKenzie, J.S., Clark, M.M., Kothera, R., and Benson, C. *Behavior Modification of Children with Learning Disabilities Using Grades as Token Reinforcers.* Unpublished mimeographed manuscript. Department of Human Development, University of Kansas, 1967.

McKenzie, H.S., Egner, A.N., Knight, M.F., Perelman, P.F., Schneider, B.J., and Garvin, J.S. "Training Consulting Teachers to Assist Elementary Teachers in the Management and Education of Handicapped Children." *Exceptional Children* 37 (1970): 137-143.

Meacham, M.L. "Reinforcement Theory as a Basis for Clinical School Psychology." *Psychology in the Schools* 5 (1968): 114-117.

Michael, J., and Meyerson, L. "A Behavioral Approach to Human Control." In *Control of Human Behavior,* edited by R. Ulrich, T. Stachnik, and J. Mabry, pp. 23-31. Glenview, Ill.: Scott, Foresman, 1966.

Morice, H.O. "The School Psychologist as a Behavioral Consultant: A Project in Behavior Modification in a Public School Setting." *Psychology in the Schools* 5 (1968): 253-261.

Mowrer, O.H. "Too Little and Too Late." *International Journal of Psychiatry* 7 (1969): 536-556.

Nolen, P.A., Kunzelmann, H.P., and Haring, N.G. "Behavioral Modification in a Junior High Learning Disabilities Classroom." *Exceptional Children* 3 (1967): 163-168.

Panda, K.C. "Effects of Social Reinforcement, Locus of Control, and Cognitive-Style on Concept Learning Among Educable Mentally Retarded Children." *Experimental Publications System,* June 1971, 12, Ms. No. 475-34.

Parton, D.A., and Ross, A.O. "Social Reinforcement of Children's Motor Behavior: A Review." *Psychological Bulletin* 64 (1965): 65-73.

Paul, G.L. "Behavior Modification Research: Design and Tactics." In *Behavior Therapy,* edited by C.M. Franks, pp. 29-62. New York: McGraw-Hill, 1969.

Portes, A. "On the Emergence of Behavior Therapy in Modern Society." *Journal of Consulting and Clinical Psychology* 36 (1971): 303-313.

Poteet, J.A. *The School Psychologist as a Modifer of Behavior — Teacher Behavior, That Is.* Paper presented in the symposium "Assessment and Management of Aggressive and Disruptive Behavior in the Classroom" at the annual meeting of the National Council on Measurement in Education, New York, February 5, 1971.

Poteet, J.A. *Behavior Modification: An Approach for Individual and Group Management.* Mimeographed. Diagnostic Teaching Center, Indianapolis Public Schools, Indianapolis, Indiana, 1970.

Premack, D. "Reinforcement Theory." In *Nebraska Symposium on Motivation,* edited by D. Levine, pp. 123-188. Lincoln: University of Nebraska Press, 1965.

Psychology Today: An Introduction. Del Mar, Calif.: CRM Books, 1970, pp. 118-119.

Risley, T.R., and Baer, D.M. "Operant Conditioning: Develop Is a Transitive Active Verb." In *Review of Child Development Research: Social Influence and Social Action.* Vol. 3. (In press.)

Roach, E.G., and Kephart, N.C. *The Purdue Perceptual-Motor Survey.* Columbus, Ohio: Charles E. Merrill Publishers, 1966.

Rogers, C. *Freedom to Learn.* Columbus, Ohio: Charles E. Merrill Publishers, 1969.

Ross, A.O. "The Application of Behavior Principles in Therapeutic Education." *Journal of Special Education* 1 (1967): 275-286.

Sattler, H.E., and Swoope, K.S. "Token System: A Procedural Guide." *Psychology in the Schools* 7 (1970): 383-386.

Scheflen, A.E. "Analysis of the Thought Model Which Persists in Psychiatry." *Psychosomatic Medicine* 20 (1958): 235-241.

Shaw, R.L., and Uhl, N.P. "Control of Reinforcement and Academic Achievement." *Journal of Educational Research* 64 (1971): 226-228.

Skinner, B.F. "Operant Behavior." *American Psychologist* 18 (1963): 503-515.

Stott, D.H. "Behavioral Aspects of Learning Disabilities: Assessment and Remediation." *Experimental Publication System,* April 1971, 11, Ms. No. 400-36.

Streff, J. Workshop on Vision Development. Presented to Diagnostic Teaching Center, Indianapolis Public Schools, Indianapolis, Indiana, October, 1971.

Stuart, R.B. *Trick of Treatment: How and When Psychotherapy Fails.* Champaign, Ill.: Research Press, 1970.

Tyler, V.O., Jr., and Brown, G.D. "Token Reinforcement of Academic Performance with Institutionalized Delinquent Boys." *Journal of Educational Psychology* 59 (1968): 164-168.

Watson, L.S. *Application of Operant Conditioning Techniques to Institutionalized Severely and Profoundly Retarded Children.* Mimeographed. Western Reserve University and Columbus State School, Ohio. No date.

Whitman, M., and Whitman, J. "Behavior Modification in the Classroom." *Psychology in the Schools* 20 (1971): 176-186.

Wolf, M.M., Hanley, E.L., King, L.A., Lachowicz, J., and Giles, D.K. "The Timer-Game: A Variable Interval Contingency for the Management of Out-of-Seat Behavior." *Exceptional Children* 37 (1970): 113-117.

Wolf, M., and Risley, T. *Analysis and Modification of Deviant Child Behavior.* Paper presented at the meeting of the American Psychological Association, Washington, D.C., 1967.

Wolpe, J.W. "Forward." In *Trick or Treatment: How and When Psychotherapy Fails,* by R.B. Stuart. Champaign, Ill.: Research Press, 1970.

Yellon, S.L., and Scott, R.O. *A Strategy for Writing Objectives.* Dubuque, Iowa: Kendall-Hunt Publishers, 1970.

Zimmerman, E.H., and Zimmerman, J. "The Alteration of Behavior in a Special Classroom Situation." In *Control of Human Behavior,* edited by R. Ulrick, T. Stachnick, and J. Mabry, pp. 94-96. Glenview, Ill.: Scott, Foresman, 1966.

Index